Fly Fishing

for

STRIPED BASS

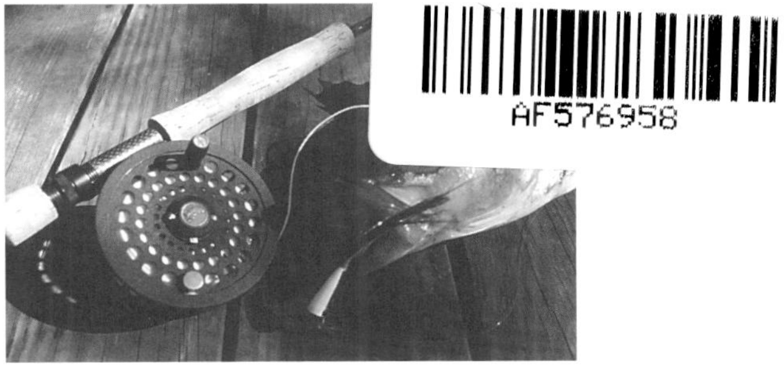

A MINI-BOOK BY
JOE BRUCE

Published by
K&D Limited, Inc.

Published by
K&D Limited, Inc.
14834 Old Frederick Road
Woodbine, MD 21797
410-489-4967

Printed in the United States of America

ISBN 0-9637161-2-3

Library of Congress Cataloging-in-Publication Data

Bruce, Joe, 1946–
Fly fishing for striped bass : a mini-book / by Joe Bruce.
p. cm.
ISBN 0-9637161-2-3
1. Striped bass fishing. 2. Salt water fly fishing. I. Title
SH691.S7B78 1997
799.1'7732—dc21 97-11155
CIP

Photos by author unless otherwise noted.

Cover and text design by K&D Limited, Inc.

Contents

More women are starting to enjoy this sport. Here's my wife, Barb, with a nice light tackle striper.

Bill Kehring

Hank Holland with a typical "schoolie" striper. Plenty of fun on a 4-weight rod.

ACKNOWLEDGEMENTS

I want to thank all of the many generous friends and fly tyers who have given me information and ideas, but I especially want to thank my wife Barbara for being my best friend and fishing companion over the years. She's a heck of a good fly tyer, too! Thanks also to my fishing buddy and shop assistant Hank Holland, for encouragement and editorial assistance on this project. Without his help, this book would not have been written. A special friend I want to single out is Lefty Kreh. Through the years, he's been great to fish with, and has always been ready to answer questions, exchange ideas and to give support.

Friends are precious things to have, and I'm very lucky to have so many.

Bill May

Lefty and myself on the Chesapeake with Capt. Kevin Josenhans out of Crisfield, MD.

Kevin Weber

Joe and Hank head for where the fish are.

Preface

I have been fishing with a fly rod since I was sixteen years old, and have never lost my desire to fish with the "long rod." Although most people associate fly fishing with trout, the variety of fishing is boundless. Whether you enjoy fishing for panfish in ponds, bass in rivers, tarpon on the flats or shark in the ocean, they all can be successfully lured to a fly. Fly fishing has always been one of my greatest joys, next to my wife and family.

As much as I love to fish, another of my pleasures has been sharing my experience and accumulated knowledge with my fellow fly fishermen. At my fly shop, *The Fisherman's Edge* in Baltimore, Maryland, I try my best to educate our customers and help them understand the variety of techniques that can increase their success rate with the fly rod. It occurred to me that a series of mini-books such as this one would be a good way to get more people introduced to wider-ranging styles of fly fishing. With the kind of information presented here, I hope to make your fly fishing experiences happier and more fruitful ones.

Hank Holland

Fly Fishing for Striped Bass is part of a series of books on flies and fishing techniques for specific fish in certain types of water.

Hank Holland

My desire for tying flies is just as strong today as it was at age sixteen.

The books are based on our experience not only in the Chesapeake Bay and surrounding area, but on many trips in various parts of the country and the Caribbean. They are intended to serve as a source of "getting started" information about fly fishing for species "beyond" trout. I've found that expanding my customers' fishing horizons has re-kindled many a flagging interest level. I hope you are encouraged as well.

Many of the fly patterns are of my design or incorporate modifications to existing patterns. Some are from other fly tyers and fisherman who have generously let me share their work in the hope that our collective experience can help make your fishing as rewarding as ours has been.

Good luck, and have fun fishing,

Joe Bruce

Chapter 1
THE STRIPED BASS

courtesy Bill May

What is the most popular large saltwater gamefish? What fish is most available to the greatest number of fishing enthusiasts? What fish is practically synonymous with the Chesapeake Bay, Cape Cod and Martha's Vineyard? Of course, the answer is the striped bass, which in waters below New Jersey is locally called "rockfish."

Stripers reach great weights; the world record was caught in New Jersey in 1992, and weighed 78 lb. 2 oz. The largest recorded fish was 125 pounds from Edenton, North Carolina in 1891. The fly rod record is a 64 lb. 8 oz. monster, taken on 12 lb. test in Smith, Oregon.

They are powerful, aggressive and generally are willing to bite. This is one of their great appeals, as they are relatively easy to catch using a variety of different fishing techniques.

In particular, they are great fare on the fly rod. They can be caught at times in water so shallow that their backs will show. They are also structure oriented like most predatory fish. They are opportunists, taking whatever food is the most abundant at the time, so they can be caught on a variety of flies from streamers and crab imitations to popping bugs.

Fly fishing for stripers is not a new sport. Tom Loving of Baltimore was fishing for stripers with a fly rod back in the 1920s. The "Loving Bass Fly" was the forerunner of the modern "Seaducer" fly. The late Joe Brooks was throwing the "long wand" at these fish in the 40s. The modern gurus of saltwater fly fishing like Lefty Kreh on the East Coast and Dan Blanton on the West Coast have been doing it for years.

Bill May

A perfect day on the Bay. . . no wind and plenty of stripers.

Stripers also adapt well to freshwater. In the lakes of Marion and Moultry in South Carolina, stripers have grown to over 50 lbs. Conveniently, the fishing techniques that are used in the salt will work equally well on the landlocked striper.

If you are new to saltwater fly fishing, you will find the information presented in this book will help you get started on the right track. I promise you that you'll thoroughly enjoy making the striper another fish that you can catch with your fly rod. They won't disappoint you with their willingness to take a fly and their ability to give you a fight you'll remember.

Nature of the Striped Bass

Though the striper is considered an anadromous fish, they migrate for two reasons: one is for the purpose of spawning and the other is a movement along the coast of New England and Canada. The latter migration is puzzling. No scientific research explains these movements, but fish over two years old will make the northward journey from the Chesapeake and Delaware Bays. This is not a recently recognized phenomenon. Early American literature addressed the striper

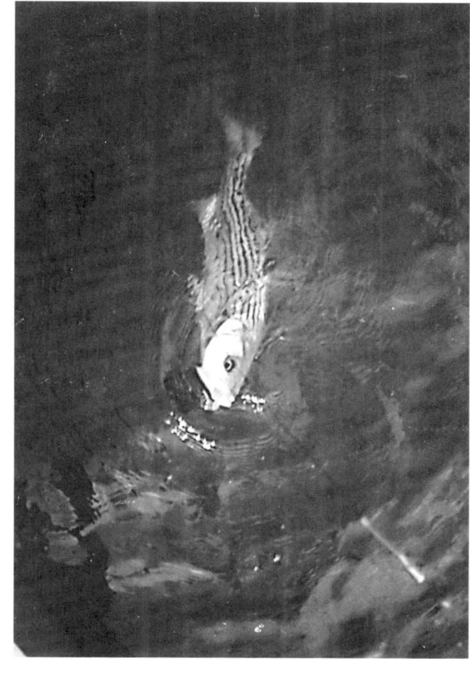

Bill May

as early as 1623, noting that the Plymouth colonists caught stripers for food and also used them for fertilizer, due to the abundance of the species.

A point of interest. Soon after the colonists landed on Plymouth, they realized the obvious value of this resource by passing an act of the General Court of Massachusetts Bay Colony, in 1639, which ordered that neither cod nor striped bass could be used as fertilizer for their crops. It is amazing that some state governments still haven't realized that these fish are a resource that needs protection from over-harvesting by commercial interests.

The original range of the striper was restricted to the Atlantic Coast until 1879, when the state of California and the United States Government planted them around Monterey. Through the years, they moved steadily north into Oregon. Farther east, they now range from Florida to the St. Lawrence and from the Gulf of Mexico to Louisiana. They are a coastal oriented fish rarely found more than a few miles from shore.

The striper grows to a moderate size and can live more than twenty years. The females are sexually mature by their fourth year at a length of 18-24 inches and 4-6 pounds. The male is mature by the second year, and all the males are ready by their third year. The larger and older the female, the more eggs are produced at spawning. So there definitely is a reason to allow the larger "cows" to live and produce. Females can spawn for as many as fourteen years, producing from 65,000 to 5,000,000 eggs a year. Spawning takes place in spring and can last as long as a month in brackish or freshwater. It was long believed that spawning would start when the water temperatures reached 55-65 degrees, but the last two great spawns in the Chesapeake had cooler water temperatures. The eggs are free floating in the current and there is no parental care. The fry hatch in about three days and live on their egg sacs for a few more days and then start eating small crustaceans and larva.

Habitat

Stripers are predators and are generally the largest species in their home waters, be it salt or freshwater. They are structure oriented, using this structure for ambush and security.

Looking for stripers in saltwater is relatively easy. Look for them where deep water comes close to the shore. This is not written in blood, only emphasized, but it is the first place to look when you're in new waters. Pay attention to the tidal flow and check out areas where structure is perpendicular to the tidal movement. If this area is near deep water, chances are that at some time stripers will be there looking for food. The disturbed water caused by tidal flows, called "tidal rips," are obvious areas where stripers will be hiding.

Structure such as piers, bridges, pilings and breakwaters are all areas that need to be investigated. People say jokingly that rockfish got their name because they like to stay around rocks, but there is a lot of truth in that. If there are rocks in the vicinity, near deep water, there should be rockfish lurking around the structure looking for their next meal.

Food And Prey

We've pointed out that stripers are opportunists who will take advantage of the most prevalent food source at the time. They will eat aquatic worms, crabs, minnows, shrimp and, of course, other fish. In freshwater, crawfish will be added to the menu.

In general, stripers feed in low light conditions. They like mornings and evenings, and will feed longer on overcast and rainy days. In tidal waters, a moving tide at such times generally creates the best fishing.

In the bays and tributaries the rockfish have a "grocery store" that is quite diversified, depending on the time of year. In the spring they will feed on minnows and grass shrimp that hang around the dead grass beds as well as around pilings and piers. In early summer, aquatic worms appear. They are sometimes called clam worms, or in the northern areas, cinder worms. They are numerous, and run in size from 1/2 inch up to 12 inches long. When stripers are after worms, they do much of their feeding at night and become very hard to catch on anything but a worm pattern.

Bill May

A nice Crisfield schoolie caught on a *Bruce's Bay Anchovy.*

Also in early summer, alewives, blue-back herring and menhaden become plentiful. These bait fish enter the bays in late spring and advance northward as the water warms. They run from 4 inches to as much as 12 inches long and represent a substantial meal for the fish. Large streamer flies are the norm when the stripers are chasing these bait fish.

As the summer progresses, the bay anchovy appears. It is the most abundant baitfish in the bay, and runs around one-half inch to two inches long. When rockfish are "breaking" while chasing schools of prey near the surface, the bay anchovy is the primary bait that you see scattering. Another prevalent, and similar, baitfish at this time is the spearing or "glass minnow" or silverside. These bait fish run from 2 to 4 inches long, and can be a significant food source.

Crabs, shrimp and eels are all forage for the rockfish through the summer and into late fall. In the colder weather, minnows and gizzard shad (mud shad) become the primary winter bait.

Again, stripers are opportunistic, and larger fish eat smaller ones. It's a tough world they live in, and just about any fish can become prey for a larger one. The biggest and fastest predators are the kings of their environment.

Bill Kollmer in the Baltimore Harbor shows off the catch of the day. Sometimes stripers can be caught right under our noses.

Look for stripers where deep water is near shore. If I took two more steps, I would be in 14′ of water.

Chapter 2
TACKLE

Rods

The type of fishing you want to do will determine what size fly rod you choose. If you like to catch a lot of fish, and size isn't the major priority, the smaller fly rods from 3-weight to 6-weight will fill the bill. If, on the other hand, you want to go after bigger fish, then the rod of choice would be an 8-weight up to a 10-weight. The bigger rods will, of course, fling the larger flies which are frequently used. Light rods can certainly subdue large fish, but the fight will be a long one; it will probably exhaust the fish (especially when the water is warm and low in oxygen) and greatly decrease its chance of survival. You *do* usually practice catch-and-release, don't you?

One of my fishing buddies, Joe Price, with a nice striper from the Baltimore harbor.

Length is a fundamental criteria to consider, for a couple of reasons. All rods are levers, and a longer lever is more efficient. In the saltwater environment longer casts are the norm, and a longer rod will help achieve this. Also, a longer rod will usually give you better lifting qualities than a shorter one. This is because the longer rod must have a larger butt diameter to carry the line weight for which it is designed. Rods from 8'-6" to 9 feet long are a good choice.

In the smaller sizes, a typical trout rod will work just fine (keeping in mind our guidelines about length). There need not be any changes to accommodate their use in saltwater, but if you are making your own, or customizing one, larger than normal guides can help. Also, if you have a wooden reel seat, you will want to be especially careful to wash any salt deposits off with fresh water. You must dry it well before storing it in a case.

Larger rods, from 8-weights and up, *should* be equipped with larger stripper guides as well as larger snake guides. The reel seat should be all metal, for strength and durability, and also needs to be fitted with a fighting butt. The larger guides and the fighting butt are musts. The bigger guides help the larger line diameter to slide through better, thus giving you longer casts for the same amount of casting force. The fighting butt helps in fighting fish by allowing you to put the butt of the rod against your hip or belly to create more fighting leverage. It also eliminates the problem of the reel getting caught in your clothing, and it extends the area your cranking hand can use.

The fighting butt need not be very long. Two inches is sufficient. The use of a fixed or removable butt is up to you. The only advantage to the removable butt is that it will fit in most rod tubes a little better when not in place. The disadvantage is that you can misplace the butt during your travels. I often wonder where all that lost gear winds up. One day I'm going to find the treasure island of lost fishing gear and become a rich man (or at least a man with a very large tackle box).

The right tackle takes the worry out of the equation between quarry and fisherman, concentrating on the fight alone.

Getting back to rods, any of the modern graphite fly rods will get the job done. The choice of fast, moderate or slow actions is very much an individual preference. The *most* important thing you can do is to try a variety of rods in the size that you want. You must see for yourself which one does the best job for you. Like many people, you may be afraid that you won't be able to tell a difference between them, but I assure you that you can. The one that feels best to you is the one that's right. Friends often tend to recommend a certain rod, but that's not really doing you a favor. Another person's casting style might not suit yours, and you're the one who'll be using it! Purchase the rod that works better for *you.*

In saltwater fishing, opportunities can come quickly, and having more than one rod on hand can change a chance into a success. Having one rod rigged with a floating line and a popper and one rigged with a sinking fly line and a weighted fly will allow an almost instant change from one fishing style to the other. If your budget doesn't allow this, there are other alternatives which will at least save on reel and spare spool costs; they might not be as fast, but they will make a little less impact on your wallet. We will discuss them in a later section.

Reels

There is more written about reels than any other tools of fly fishing (other than lines). I guess this is understandable considering that there are some 84 manufacturers of fly reels on the market. We'll try to clear up any confusion.

What do you need to fish the salt? Again, it's based on your fishing goals. Are you going to fish for smaller fish with your trout gear, or are you going to look for the "big boys." A great many people want to do both.

While many people assume that you need special reels for saltwater, most modern fly reels will work just fine. If you are targeting smaller fish, your trout reels will do the job. When you are done fishing, wash your gear under warm water with mild soap. Dry and lubricate where you normally would for the freshwater and you have it. Though not all reels are anodized, soap and water will

Some of the reels I use.

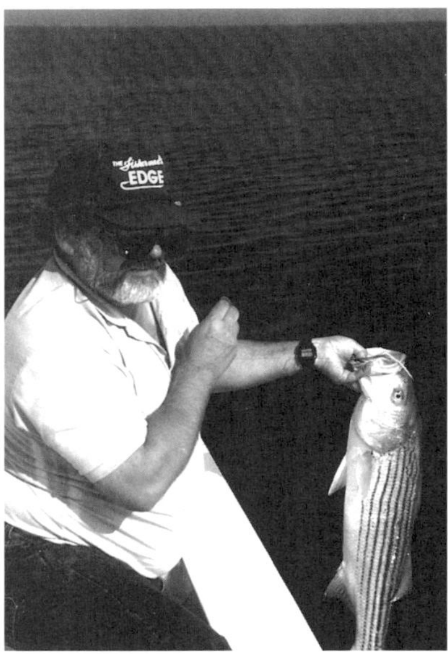

take the salt off. A camel hair brush or soft toothbrush worked around the reel and spool will usually do the trick.

When you go after the big boys using larger rods (from 8-weight up), a larger capacity reel is in order. You don't have to spend an arm and a leg to purchase a serviceable saltwater reel. Cortland, Scientific Angler and STH make reels that won't cause you to take out a second mortgage. These reels cost from $100 to $240, with extra spools running at around half of the reel cost. The best reels will cost more, and they *are* better, but less expensive ones will get the job done, too.

A reel for stripers should handle a minimum of 150 yards of twenty pound test backing with the appropriate size line-weight. This is enough capacity to handle any striper that swims. The drag system should be reasonably large and smooth, staying smooth even when wet.

To reinforce a lesson that you probably have already learned, remember that buying the best equipment that you can afford is always the best policy. Better rods, reels and lines will hold up over the years, and generally carry a lifetime warranty. Also consider that you may want to use the tackle on other quarry where better equipment *will* be needed, like small tarpon, bonefish, false albacore, etc.

Lines

You *should* invest your money in the best lines that you can afford. Better lines have better and harder finishes which will aid in making longer casts, and which will be more durable as well. There are literally hundreds of lines on the market when you consider the range of sizes as well as the variety of floating, sinking, sink-tips, etc. What are the best lines for striper fishing? The choices can be overwhelming, so we'll try to simplify things a bit.

Part of my assortment of lines.

To start with basics, there are two lines that will handle 90% of your striper fishing. These are a floating line and some sort of sinking line. Ninety-five percent of your fishing will take place under the surface, so we'll look at the sinking lines first.

Let's discuss the sinking lines for the larger rods. The most used sinking lines on the market are the "T" series lines by Jim Teeny, a West Coast steelhead fly fisherman, manufactured under the label of Teeny Nymph Lines. Although these lines were first designed by Mr. Teeny for steelhead they soon found great acceptance by the saltwater fly fraternity as the choice sinking line for the salt. These lines are designated by grain weight rather than by typical line-weight. Below is a table of "T" series line that will work with the different size rods.

TEENY "T" SERIES NYMPH LINES		
MODEL	ROD WEIGHT	SINK RATE
T-130	3-4-5 wt. rods	4.0 IPS
T-200	5-6-7 wt. rods	5.5 IPS
T-300	8-9-10 wt. rods	6.5 IPS
T-400	10-11-12 wt. rods	8.0 IPS
T-500	13-14-15 wt. rods	9.0 IPS

All these lines cast much like a shooting head. They all have a 24-foot high density sinking front end with a fine diameter floating running line behind. All you have to do is get the head and about 3 feet of the running line outside of the rod tip and make your forward cast. It is counter-productive to extend the head out any further to make the cast, as the thin running line won't support the heavy sinking section. For rod weights from 8 to 10, the T-300 will be the right choice. For the 5- and 6-weights, the T-200 will do a great job.

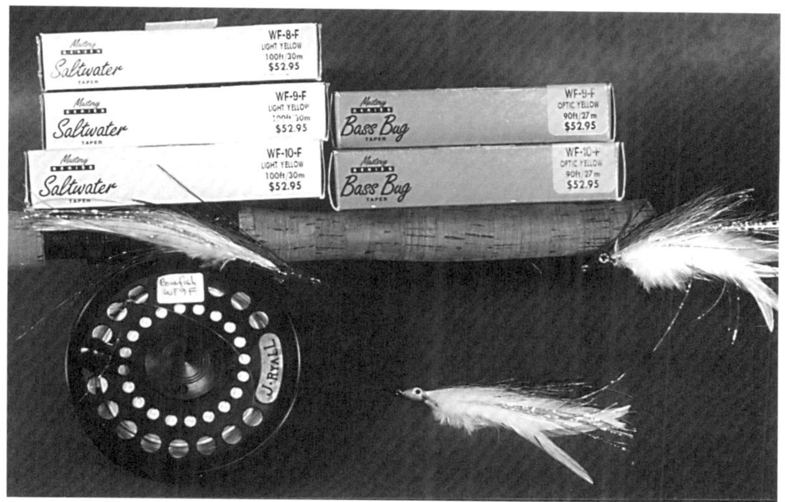

Some floating lines that will handle larger flies.

The other line that you must have is a floater. There are standard weight-forward lines, saltwater lines, shooting lines and some specialty lines like Cortland's XRL shooting tapers and Scientific Anglers' new Striper Lines.

What line should you choose? The first question you have to answer is where and at what time of the year will you be fishing these lines. Why does this matter? Because of the varying nature of fishing locales, line manufacturers have developed "saltwater lines" designed especially for the summer and tropical heat. These lines will not get soft and limp laying on the deck of a boat in 100 degree temperatures with the sun trying to fry the line as well as your brain. The drawback with these lines is that they get pretty stiff in cooler climates; so when it gets cold, they will retain a coil and be very hard to manage. If colder climate fishing is in your cards, then a standard weight-forward or bass-taper line will be the best choice for your saltwater needs. The Wulff TT saltwater tapers work very well in cool weather, too. The stiffness factor is also true for Cortland's XRL Striper Lines and Scientific Anglers' Striper Lines. although the latter seems to be manageable in the cold. These lines have a braided nylon core with a super hard finish on the tapered 43-foot heads. The long head and thin running line makes a great choice for pounding out long casts, but remember the weather factor.

At the end of the discussion on rods, we noted a less expensive way to handle the cost of reels and extra spools. The alternative is to use a shooting head system. This will allow you to purchase a better reel, because you don't need extra spools. The setup consists of your backing, a thin running line (this can be floating line or nylon braided line) with a loop in the outer end, and a 30 foot shooting head. These heads are the same front sections that come with a full line, but are fitted with a loop at the rear end to allow changing via a loop-to-loop connection with the running line. Heads are available in floating, intermediate sinking (a slow sink-

of Bill May

Deepwater and a nice striper will put a bend in a nine-weight rod.

ing head, usually 1-1/2 inches per second), full-sinking or 10-foot sink-tips with a 20-foot floating head behind. The sinking lines come in all descent rates, but the best choice is the fastest available, something around 6-1/2 to 7 inches per second. This line is the real work-horse, since even in shallower water you can simply retrieve faster or make shorter casts to the edges of the drops.

Speaking of shallows, if the budget will allow it, an intermediate line can be very helpful. This slower sinking line, about 1-1/2 to 2 inches per second, will allow you to keep the fly suspended off the bottom and still give you time to keep the fly in the target area longer.

With these three lines (fast-sinking, floating and intermediate) you can fish 98% of the situations that arise for striper fishing with heavy-weight rods.

If you decide that you would like to use your trout gear on the smaller stripers found in the bays and tributaries, you only need to

purchase two lines to handle 98% of the fishing situations. What you'll need are a 5-foot sink-tip and a T-130 or T-200 Teeny Nymph line, depending on your rod weight.

The 5-foot sink-tip is the first choice. Both Cortland Line Co. and Teeny Nymph Lines make 5-foot sink tips. They come in weights from 3 to 10, with Cortland starting at 5-weight. Both have very fast sink rates at 6-1/2 to 7 inches per second. These lines work well around the shore line where you're casting to water no deeper than 4 feet. A 12-inch striper on a 3- or 4-weight rod will give a good account of himself; you might even decide to give up trout fishing — at least part of the time! These smaller stripers are a tremendous amount of fun on the small rods.

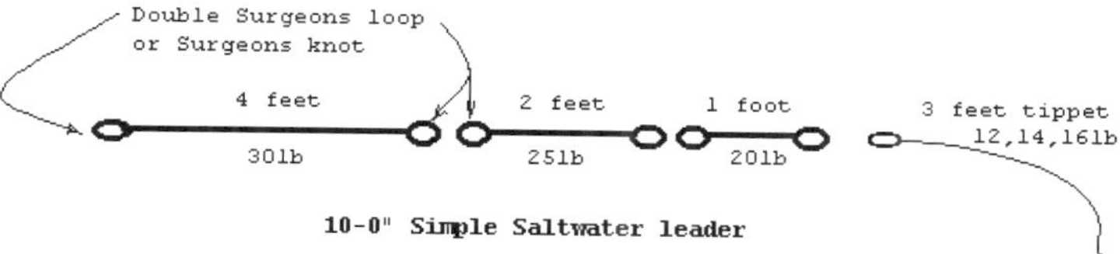

Leaders

Leaders for stripers need not be complicated. Stripers aren't leader shy. For floating lines, you can simply cut about five to six feet of the size monofilament that you feel will do the job. I usually use from 12 pound to 20 pound for my fishing. If you need a little more control, then a simple three-part leader will work. Start with 4 feet of 30 lb. test, next add 2 feet of 25 lb., then 1 foot of 20 lb., and finally 2 to 3 feet of your tippet. That's it.

For sinking lines it's even simpler. Just pull off 3 to 4 feet of monofilament and you are ready to fish. The shorter leader will keep the fly near the bottom, since that's where your line is. You obviously have more control if your fly does not stray too far from your line. Again, these fish aren't leader shy and the short leader won't deter them.

As an overall point of view about tackle concerns and requirements, buy the best that you can afford, but keep the terminal tackle simple.

How do you put the backing, line and leaders on the reel? What type of knots do you need to know? We won't provide knot illustrations, since there are many references, both as complete books and as pamphlets that come with your line. A good knot

book is not a useless expense; learning good knots at home is invaluable in the field. The main thing that needs to be said about knots is to *tie good ones* , bad knots are always bad knots. Take the time to tie a good knot, since this is your weakest link between you and the fish.

There are only a few knots needed to handle fly fishing gear, some you probably already know. The first one is the connection between the fly reel arbor and the backing. I prefer to make a *perfection* or *surgeons* loop knot, loop the standing part of the line through it, and throw this over the spool to form a *clove hitch*. On some reels where the spool is not easily removed you can use an *arbor knot*. After winding on the backing, you need to make a decision. Do you attach the fly line to the backing with a permanent knot or do you form a loop in the backing and form a loop in the end of the fly line and attach these together with a "quick loop" method. Either method is fine. If you decide to make a permanent knot, an *Albright* will give good service. This knot will encompass the fly line into a double line with the backing wrapped around both lines. Although nail knots are often recommended for this connection, they rely on the coating on the fly line to hold the knot. This is not as solid a knot for the salt, where at any time a larger fish might make your fly its next meal. The *Albright* will handle these situations, with confidence.

The *loop to loop* method of attaching the backing and fly line has one advantage. You don't need extras reel spools with this system, you can unwind the fly line and put on another. Saving the empty line spools from your orignal purchase will give you the container to store the line.

After the fly line and backing are attached you will need to make the transition from the fly line to the leader. A twelve inch piece of forty pound stiff monofiliament constructed to form a *butt loop* will make this connection. Fasten one end of the stiff mono to the fly line with an *Albright* knot. Put a loop in the other end with either a *non-slip loop* or a *double surgeon's knot.* Put a loop in the other end of your leader and use a *loop to loop* connection to fasten the leader to the *butt loop*. The only knot left is the connection between the leader and the fly. I prefer to use the *non-slip* loop here. This simple but strong knot will allow my fly to move and swing around during the retrieve, allowing more animation to my presentation.

Need help with these knots? Most good fly shops will do them for you during the purchase of the outfit or at least will show you how to tie these knots. They aren't hard, they just need to be practiced.

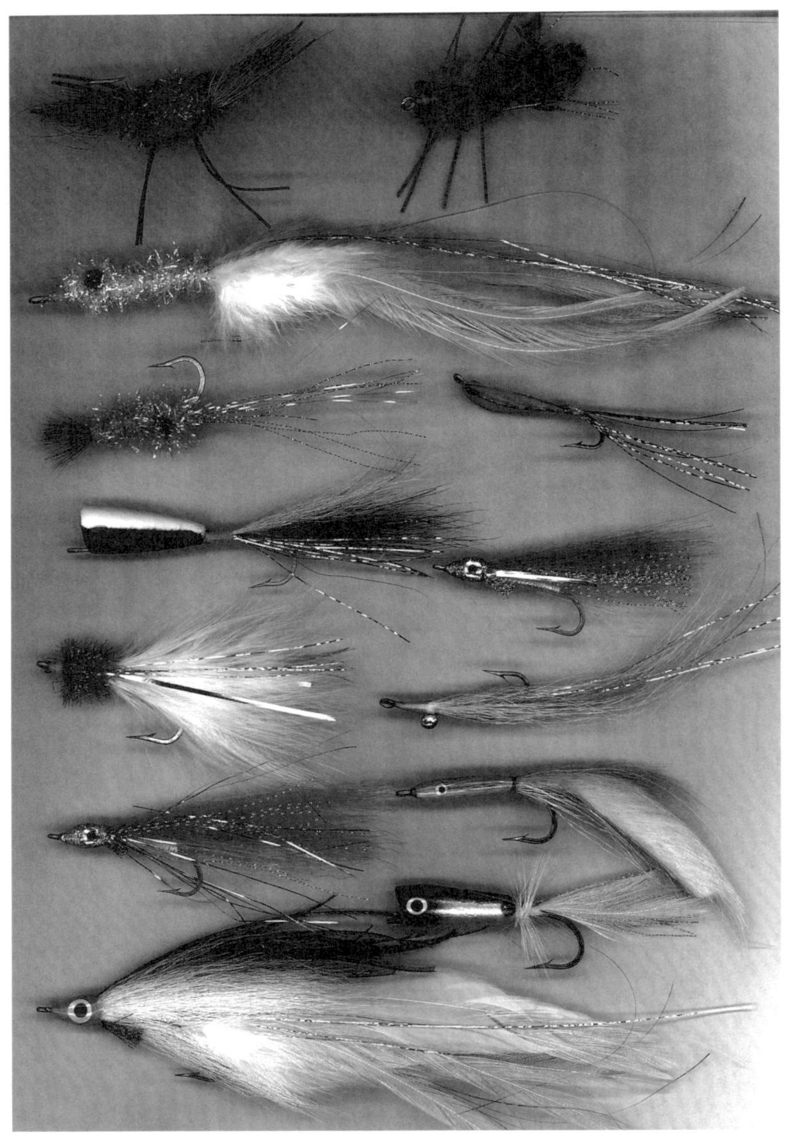

Chapter 3
FLIES AND PATTERNS

There are endless fly patterns for stripers. You may like some for certain areas, or it may be that you simply have confidence in a pattern that has worked for you in the past.

The following flies and patterns are flies that have proven to be excellent striper producers over the years. Some patterns are old standbys and some patterns are creations of mine and some of my fishing partners. Some of these are *The Fisherman's Edge's* patterns, so we will describe and illustrate them and provide tying instructions. They are time-tested and will enhance your arsenal of flies. We will also provide instructions for some other flies we like that you might not be too familiar with.

Surface Flies

Think of surface patterns, and no doubt the first fly that comes to mind is the popper. These can be made of cork, foam, living rubber, etc. They come in many different shapes. They can be bold-faced, cupped poppers that make a lot of noise and throw large amounts of the water when you strip them; they can be elongated slim poppers that make only a slight disturbance, or they can be a slider type that darts under the water on a pull. Which one do you choose? The more you striper fish, you will use all of the different shapes, but I'll tell you about my favorite.

Experience has shown that the most consistent producer is the pencil popper. This slim, elongated popper will dance, pop and quiver on the surface enticing the striper which is underneath it. What color? That's easy, *white.* Another color combination that works well is a popper painted black on the bottom and white on top. This will allow you to see the popper on the surface, as well

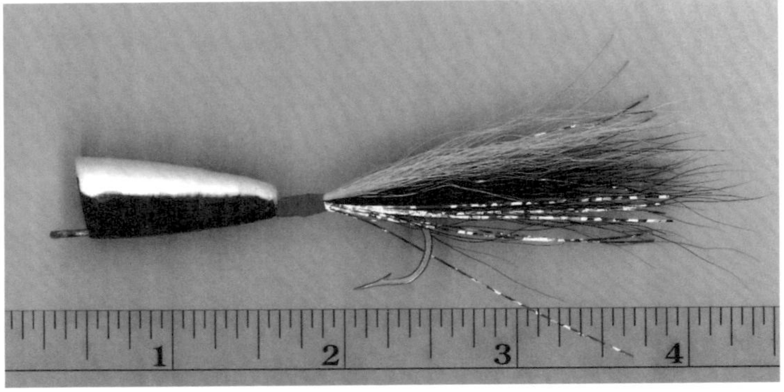

as create a better silhouette for the fish viewing it from underneath. I go so far as to add black bucktail to the exposed underside of the hook shank with white on top of the black so that I can see it. Of course a little silver tinsel is added along the way for flash.

BRUCE'S NITE & DAY POPPER

Hook:	Mustad #32669 CT- #1/0
Thread:	Fire-orange flat waxed nylon
Tail:	Black & white bucktail
Tinsel:	Silver Krystal Flash
Body:	Wapsi's saltwater pencil popper #2. Fasten body to hook shank with "Duco" cement or super glue and let dry.
Color:	Permanent black magic marker

◆ TYING INSTRUCTIONS

1. Place hook in vise and attach thread behind popper body.
2. Take a bundle of black bucktail the size of 1/4 pencil diameter and tie on the hook shank. This hair can be as long as the hook length.

3. Get about 10 strands of silver Krystal Flash and tie on one side of the hook shank and do the same to the other side. This should extend 1/4" past the bucktail.
4. Take the same amount of white bucktail and tie this on the top of the hook shank over the black bucktail.
5. Use black magic marker to paint the underside of the popper body and up the sides to half of the popper diameter.
6. Smooth out wraps, whip finish and apply head cement.

A surface strike is one of the most exciting thrills we can have when a fish takes a fly. Therefore, we all immediately think of poppers when fish are breaking. However, they are not the most productive flies for the purpose. A fly that hangs just *under* the surface will result in many more hook-ups. Also, they produce the same excitement as a surface strike; since the fly will be only a couple of inches below the surface, you will *still* see the take.

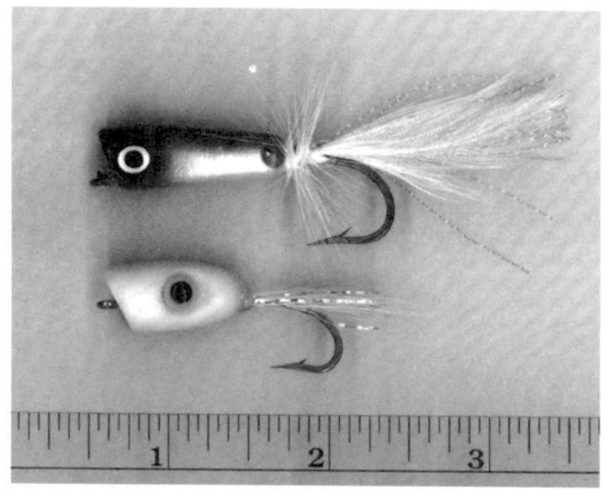

Let's illustrate this. Have you seen a school of breaking rockfish? How many baitfish do you think are *under* the water? How many are out of the water? Though there may be thousands of baitfish being driven up to the surface, there are very few actually on the surface. It's simply not natural for bait or predatory fish to be out of the water. A baitfish is vulnerable as it falls back into the water. It is isolated, and it doesn't want to be alone; there is safety in numbers. Rockfish are not the most accomplished surface feeders (they frequently miss as they try to grab the prey,) so you tend to miss a lot of fish on poppers. A fly just under the surface is a better bet.

Lefty Kreh's Red & White Streamer is a good choice under the surface on a floating or intermediate line. This fly is similar to the "Seaducer" pattern that has been around for years. It is a bushy, subsurface fly that will give the image of a large baitfish trapped at the surface. Although it was first used for smallmouth bass in the rivers, it works equally well in the salt; just add a stainless steel hook instead of a bronzed one.

The fly is a good choice when fishing shallow or when working over grass beds. Its almost neutral buoyancy will allow a slower presentation, and the tantalizing movement will sometimes bring a fish out of its hiding place.

LEFTY'S RED & WHITE STREAMER

Hook:	Mustad #34007, size #2/0
Thread:	Fire-orange flat waxed nylon
Tail:	White marabou
Tinsel:	Silver Flashabou & pearl Krystal Flash
Head:	Red Flash Chenille

◆ TYING INSTRUCTIONS

1. Place hook in vise and attach thread behind eye. Wind thread back toward hook bend about half the hook shank.
2. Attach a large bunch of white marabou at this point by throwing two loose wraps of thread around the marabou and slowly tighten the thread as you slowly let the marabou slide around the hook shank. This should be evenly dispersed. Marabou should extend past the hook bend about twice the hook length.
3. Take three or four strands each of the Flashabou and Krystal Flash and tie in on each side of the marabou, aligning it with the hook shank. Tinsel should extend beyond the marabou about 3/8".
4. At this point tie in about 4" of red Flash Chenille and wind thread to back of hook eye.
5. Wind the Flash Chenille to back of hook eye, leaving enough room to form the head.
6. Form head, whip finish and apply head cement.

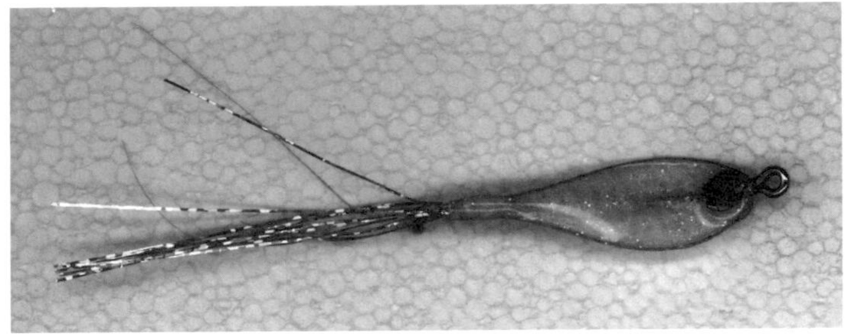

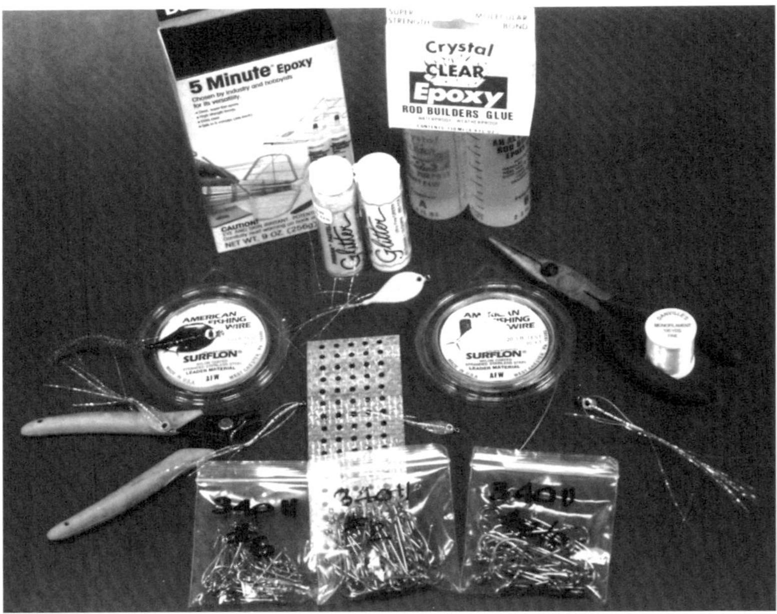

Tools and materials needed for Bruce's Epoxy Spoon Fly. At first glance it appears that you need to go to the hardware store, but other than the epozy most fly shops will carry these products.

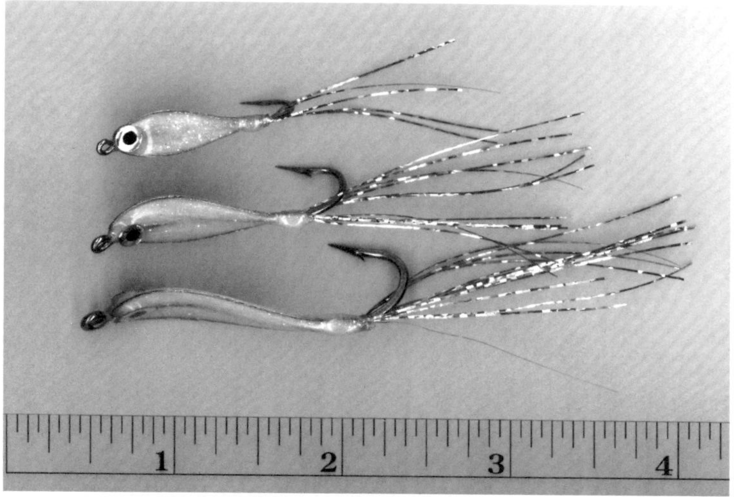

My Epoxy Spoon Fly is a fly lure created specifically to take fish that are breaking at the surface. It has the added bonus of handling bluefish and Spanish mackerel. I hated to have to change my fly each time that bluefish would show up during a surface feeding frenzy. The epoxy body holds up well to these toothy critters. Although the original fly was designed for stripers and blues, it has taken every species of fish that it was thrown at. This includes pickerel, bass, bluegill, crappie, white and yellow perch, seatrout, redfish, bonefish and false albacore, just by changing the hook size. It has also proved to work in searching situations under water — not just on breaking fish.

The body is epoxy that is colored with powder paint pigment. Successful colors are pearl, chartreuse, gold and black for night. They also have glitter added to the epoxy for extra flash.

BRUCE'S EPOXY SPOON FLY

Hook: #34011, sizes #6, #2 & #2/0

Thread: Clear fine monofilament

Tail: Holographic tinsel or flashabou of your choice

Eyes: Paste-on with black pupils over silver. For Hooks #6 & #2 use 3mm eyes. For #2/0 hooks use 4mm eyes.

Body Frame: "Surflon" nylon coated wire, 15 lb. for #6 and #2 hooks, 20 lb. for #2/0 hook

Head & Body: "Devon" Brand 5-minute epoxy with paint pigment

Glitter: Ultrafine glitter in green and soft blue manufactured by "Glick" and found in most fabric stores.

◆ TYING INSTRUCTIONS

1. Use standard width needle nose pliers to grasp the hook behind the eye with the hook point facing you and start a smooth slight bend down the hook shank, away from the hook point, to a point 1/3 way down the shank. This bend should be a smooth curve through this length.

2. Attach the mono thread behind the hook eye and advance to the bend of the hook and wind back to the hook eye.

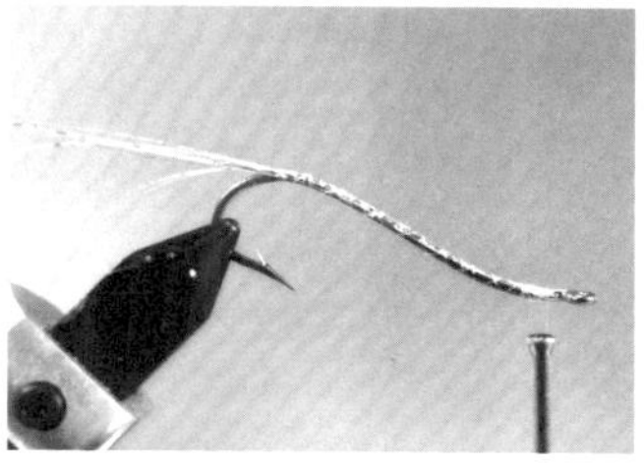

3. Cut 6 strands of holographic tinsel and tie in at the back of the hook eye. Advance thread and tinsel back to the bend of the hook, taking care to keep the tinsel on top of the hook shank. Flash should extend one hook length beyond the bend. Advance thread back to hook eye.

4. Invert hook in vise and apply the six strands of Holographic Flash to the underside of the hook shank. Again wrap tinsel to hook bend and advance thread to back of hook eye.

5. Attach about 4" of "Surflon" nylon coated steel wire behind hook eye. Wire should be perpendicular to the hook shank with equal amounts extending out each side. This is accomplished by figure-eighting around the wire and hook shank. Be careful not to kink the wire.

6. Advance the thread to a position above the hook barb and pull one side of the wire to this point and tie off, but don't cut the tag. Next bring the remaining wire to the other side and

tie down. Both wires should be along the hook shank. The width of the body is up to you.

7. Cut both wire tags a little long and continue winding the tags down, advancing the thread to the bend of the hook. Whip finish the thread at this point.

8. Attach eyes on each side of the hook shank within the wire frame at the hook eye. Do this just behind the wire tie-in point.

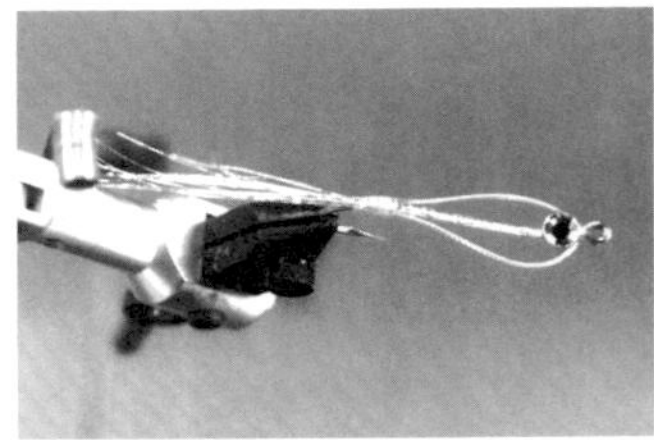

◆ APPLYING THE EPOXY

Straighten out a large paper clip to use for mixing the epoxy and applying to the frame.

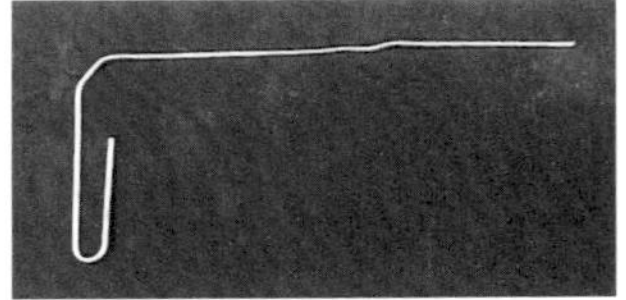

1. Mix enough epoxy to fill the body cavity. Add green and blue glitter as desired. At this point you can add the paint pigment. Powder paint works great, but you also can use acrylic or latex paint. You only need a few drops of paint or pigment to color the epoxy. Experience will tell you when the mix is right.
2. Apply the 5-minute epoxy first around the paste-on eyes on each side and then apply some epoxy to both sides of the wire tie-off point at the hook bend.

3. Get as large a dollop of epoxy as you can pick up, and lay it around the eyes and try to pull the mixture back to the hook bend. At first this will seem like it can't be done, but it will fill in. Do this one side at a time until both sides are covered.
4. Now use the paper clip to remove any excess around the center of the hook shank as well as around the paste-on eyes. By removing a little of the epoxy on the hook shank you will expose the tied-down tinsel giving the shaft a flashy lateral line on both side of the spoon. Take care to remove any excess epoxy on the paste-on eye.
5. Place the spoon on a rotating motor or in a rotating vise and turn for 5 minutes.

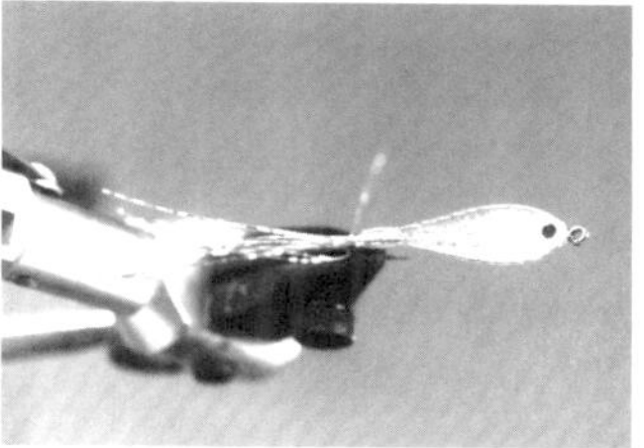

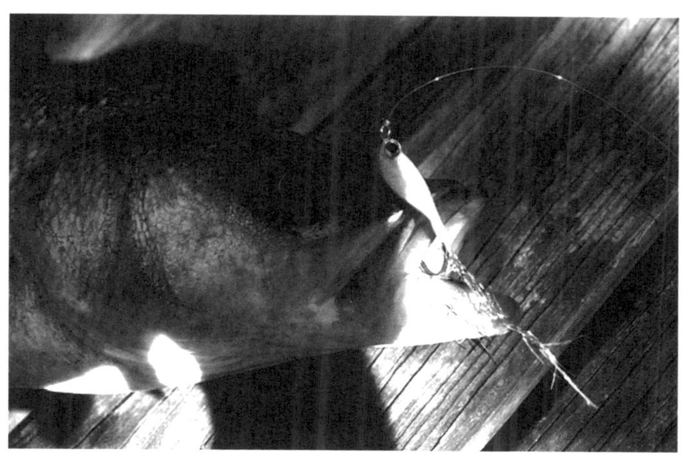

Sub-Surface Flies

The following flies are just some of the effective flies to use for stripers under the surface, but they are versatile enough to do double or triple duty from the surface to the bottom.

The best known mid-water fly by far is "Lefty's Deceiver." This combination of feathers and bucktail is probably the first choice among experienced saltwater fly fisherman. Although the Deceiver is a style of fly tying rather than a specific pattern, it, along with the best bottom bouncer fly, the "Clouser Deep Minnow," has probably accounted for more fish caught in the salt than any other pattern in the world.

This pattern is tied in about every color of the rainbow, and you'll find one that you have confidence in and will use the most. One style that has been very successful is *The Fisherman's Edge's* version of the "Lefty's Deceiver." This version carries only four saddles on the tail, a combination of white, pink and dark blue bucktail wings and paste-on eyes, with the head epoxied for durability. The combination of pink and blue on the top of the wing has the gradual blending of colors that is found on the menhaden, alewife and blue-backed herring, all of which are important Atlantic Coast baitfish. This color combo flashes that subtle purple color in the water that can't be achieved with the use of purple only.

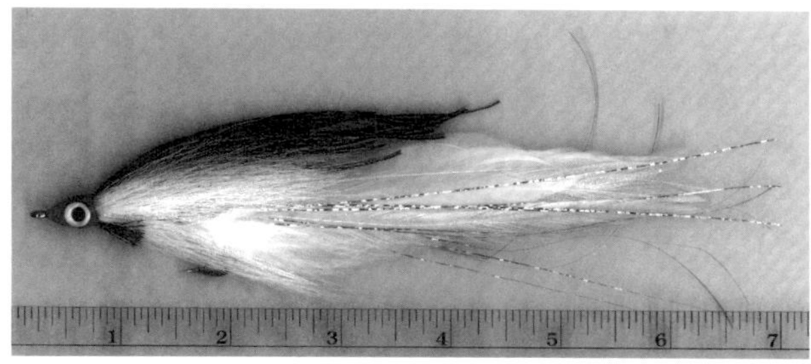

THE FISHERMAN'S EDGE'S LEFTY'S DECEIVER

Hook: Mustad #34011, sizes #2/0 & #4/0 for larger flies, Mustad #34007, size #1/0 for smaller ones.

Thread: Fire-orange flat waxed nylon

Tail: Four white saddle hackles

Tail tinsel: Six strands of silver or blue holographic tinsel

Body: Wide silver tinsel

Underwing: White bucktail

Throat: Red Krystal Flash

Overwing: Pink bucktail

Top Overwing: Blue bucktail

Back: Peacock herl

Eyes: 4mm silver back with black pupils (#2/0, #4/0) 3mm for #1/0

Head: Fire-orange thread and 5-minute epoxy

◆ TYING INSTRUCTIONS

1. Place hook in vise and attach thread behind hook eye and advance the thread to bend of hook.
2. Advance thread about 1/4" toward hook eye, this is the saddle tie in point. Prepare the four saddles by measuring the length of the saddles at the tie in point and strip off the fluff at the base of the stem. The length of the fly is up to you and the availability of longer saddles. 4" is about right for the #1/0 hooks and about 6" for the #2/0 or #4/0.
3. Marry two saddles together and tie in on the hook shank the farthest away from you with the concave side of the feathers facing you.
4. Take the other two saddles and tie them on the side nearest to you. Concave side will be away from you. Wind these saddles down to the hook bend. Take care that the saddles stay in place on each side of the hook shank.
5. Apply the 6 strands of holographic tinsel on each side of the saddles. Tinsel should extend 3/8" beyond the tips of the saddles.
6. Advance thread to the back of the hook eye and tie in the wide flat tinsel. Wind the tinsel back to the bend of hook and then back to the hook eye and tie off.
7. Invert hook in vise and take a half of a pencil diameter (for 2/0, smaller for 1/0) of white bucktail and tie in the underbody. This bucktail should reach about half way back on the saddle.

8. Tie in the red Krystal Flash throat at the head and then turn the hook back over in the vise. The Flash should extend about 1/4" to 3/8" from the hook shank.
9. Take the same amount of pink bucktail and tie in the overbody in a position just opposite of the underbody tie in point. Option: At this point you can also tie in some more holographic tinsel if you desire. Let this extend back to the ends of the tinsel applied at the tail.
10. Repeat this with the blue bucktail.
11. Take 10 to 15 strands of peacock herl and tie this over top the blue bucktail. This should be a little shorter than the saddles. At this point the head should have a large taper, this is desired to apply the paste-on eyes.
12. Apply the 4mm (#2/0, #4/0), 3mm for #1/0 paste-on eyes on each side of the head.
13. Mix a small batch of 5-minute epoxy and cover the eyes and head of the fly. Place on rotating motor and let dry. The epoxy will be completely cured in 24 hours.

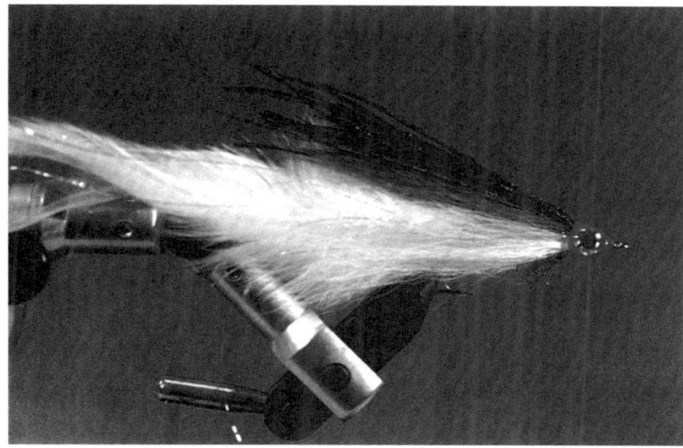

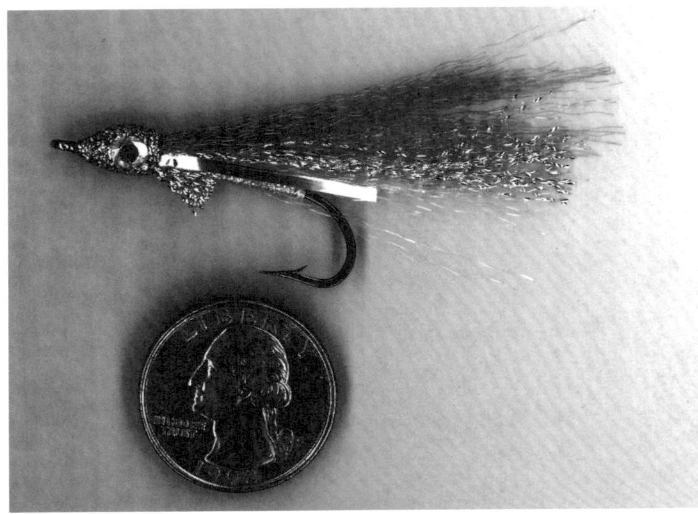

The largest population of baitfish in most bays of the Atlantic Coast are the spearing (silver sides, glass minnow) and the bay anchovy. Both of these fish have similarities, and sometimes they are mis-identified. At first glance they do look alike, but upon closer examination the anchovies don't possess the bright lateral line that the silversides have from cheek to base of tail. Instead they have a lesser defined line running from the abdomen to the tail. In addition, they have a bright silver abdomen and head that doesn't exist on the silversides. The bay anchovy is a smallish bait, being from 1 to 2-1/2 inches, while the silversides can grow to 4 inches. Both minnows carry a pale gray back with purple/pearl iridescence. The bay anchovy is a significant food source for blues and stripers during the summer and fall, and is the food source most common with breaking fish during these times.

BRUCE'S BAY ANCHOVY

Hook: Mustad #34011, Size #2

Thread: Fine clear monofilament

Body: Kreinik 1/8" pearl flat ribbon (wide holographic tinsel or Mylar tubing can be substituted)

Abdomen: Silver Krystal Flash

Overbody: Polar bear Ultrahair

Lateral Line: Wide silver tinsel

Back: Smoke Ultrahair

Iridescence: Silver Krystal Flash

Top: Dark Grey Ultrahair

Head: Silver Krystal Flash

Eye: 3mm silver/black pupil pate on eyes

Head cover: 5-minute epoxy

◆ TYING INSTRUCTIONS

1. Insert hook in vise and attach mono thread behind hook eye and wind to bend of hook.
2. Cut 4-1/2" of Kreinik ribbon and tie in at this point. Advance thread to 1/8" behind hook eye and wind the ribbon on the hook shank advancing it toward hook eye and tie off and cut at the thread position.
3. Invert hook in vise. Take about 15 to 20 strands of Krystal Flash and tie this in under the hook shank at the tie off point of the ribbon. Wind back about 1/8" and cut off the fibers about 1/4" above the hook shank. This serves as the abdomen.

4. Invert hook again to its normal position and take about 10 to 15 strands of Polar Bear Ultrahair and tie in behind hook eye. The overbody should extend past the hook bend about 1/2".
5. Take the wide silver tinsel and tie it in behind the hook eye on each side of the hook shank. Tinsel should extend to hook bend only.
6. Get the same size bundle of smoke Ultrahair and tie on top of the Polar Bear. Tie the butts a little further back than the polar bear, this will help build up the tapered head. End this at the same point as the Polar Bear.
7. Take about 8 to 10 strands of silver Krystal Flash and tie on top of the smoke Ultrahair. Extend this past the Ultrahair about 1/4".
8. Use about same amount of dark grey ultrahair and tie this down on top of the hook shank a little further back than the smoke Ultrahair. Advance thread to middle of head.
9. Take the same quantity of Krystal Flash as in step #7 and tie down on top of the bucktail and advance thread behind hook eye. Wind the tinsel down the head to the hook eye and then back to cover head completely. Wind mono thread over tinsel and cut off tags and whip finish.
10. Apply paste-on eyes to each side of head and mix epoxy and coat entire head. Place on rotating motor and let dry.

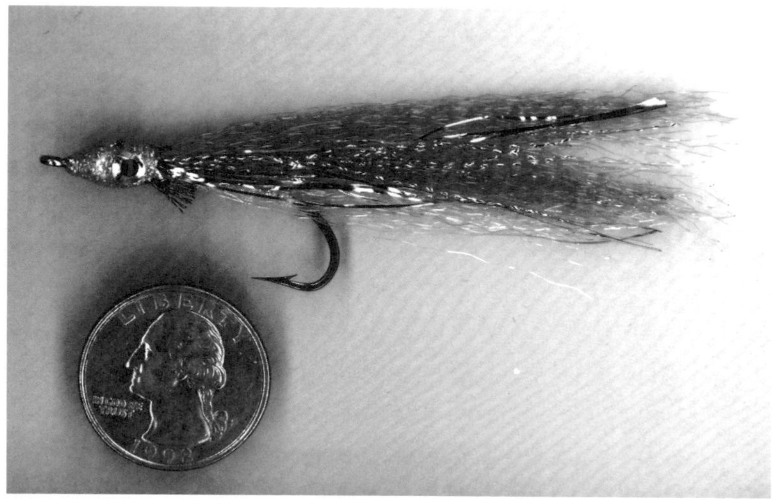

As stated above, the second most abundant baitfish on the Coast is the spearing or "glass minnow" or "silversides." Imitations of this bait have been tied for years, attempting to mimic this important food source. They have been tied with bucktail, feathers or a combination of both, all with the same glaring mistake. They are all opaque materials. *The silversides are nearly transparent.* This translucency is not achievable with opaque materials. Luckily, we have Wapsi's Supreme Hair, Spirit River and Umpqua's Super Hair and Thompson's Ultrahair. These materials are artificial hair made from nylon. They offer the translucent quality that we need to produce that critical effect in our flies.

"Bruce's Ultrahair Silversides" fly uses four colors of this material to give the image and shading of the baitfish, producing its subtle color changes from top to bottom.

BRUCE'S ULTRAHAIR SILVERSIDES

Hook: Mustad #34011, size # 2

Thread: Fine clear monofilament

Body: Kreinik 1/8" pearl ribbon

Throat: Red Krystal Flash

Underbody: Polar Bear Ultrahair or equal

Overbody: Neon pink Ultrahair or equal

Iridescence: Six strands of silver Krystal Flash and 12 to 15 strands of silver Flashabou

Overbody 2: Blue Ultrahair or equal

Back: Dark gray Ultrahair or equal

Head: Pearl Krystal Flash

Eyes: 3mm sliver/black pupil paste-on eyes

Head Cover: 5-minute epoxy

TYING INSTRUCTIONS

1. Insert hook in vise and attach mono thread behind hook eye and advance to bend of hook.
2. Cut 4 1/2" of 1/8" ribbon and tie in at the hook bend. Advance thread to 1/8" behind hook eye. Wrap ribbon on itself, advancing to hook eye and tie off and cut tag.
3. Invert hook in vise and take about 15 strands of Red Krystal Flash and tie in at the tie off point of the ribbon on the opposite side of the hook shank.
4. Invert hook in vise to its normal position and take about 12 to 15 strands of polar bear and tie in on top of the hook shank, behind the hook eye. Extend the

hair a hook length behind the hook bend. Stagger the cut ends.

5. Take the same amount of neon pink and tie in a little behind the tie-in point of the polar bear. This will start the taper for the head. Stagger cut the same length as the polar bear.
6. Tie in the Krystal Flash and Flashabou and cut off the same length as the hair.
7. Tie in the same amount of blue Ultrahair over the tinsel, taking care not to push the tinsel around the hook shank. The tinsel should remain on top. Stagger cut like the other hair.
8. Do the same thing with the dark gray Ultrahair.
9. Advance the thread to the middle of the head and tie in 6 to 8 strands of pearl Krystal Flash. Wind the flash around the head criss-crossing the material to cover the entire head. End with the flash behind the hook eye, but don't cut off. Pull the flash to the top of the head and tie down with the tying thread advancing the material to the back of the head. Cut off tinsel and smooth the head with the thread, if needed.
10. Apply the 3mm paste-on eyes on each side of the head.
11. Mix a small amount of epoxy and cover head. Rotate and let dry.

Bottom Bouncers

The bottom bouncing flies are the top producing flies in a fisherman's arsenal, for the simple reason that fish spend 90% or more of their time on or near the bottom. It stands to reason that a fly that stays in the same area will produce strikes.

Although the following flies are described as bottom searching patterns, they can also be used anywhere in the water column, as can most any subsurface fly.

The most used bottom bouncing fly by far is the "Clouser Deep Minnow." Although the original fly was designed to catch smallmouth bass, it has become a "must-have" fly for saltwater use.

We won't give tying instruction for this fly, since it appears in just about any fly tying guide you can get your hands on, but we will give you some of the best color combinations. These flies can be tied on hooks from as small as #8 through hooks in the #5/0 range. You'll want to have a few of different sizes to match the bait size. Yes, "matching the hatch" applies to saltwater fly fishing too!

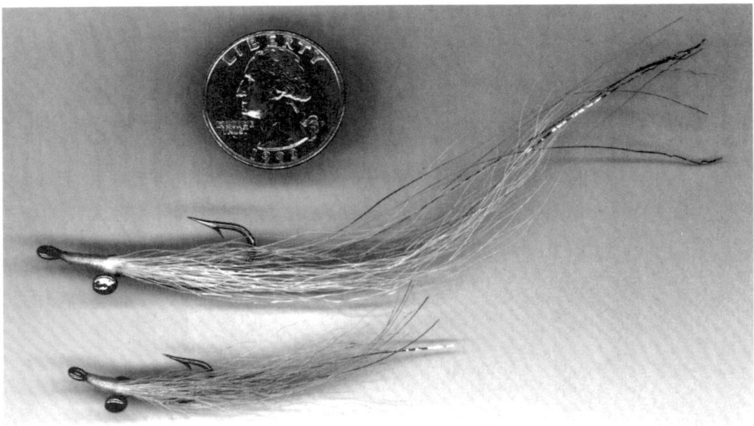

Clouser Deep Minnows, the most used bottom bouncing fly.

Some favorite color combination to have in your fly box are yellow over white, chartreuse over white, blue over white, grey over white, all white and all black for night or very low light situations. Also, tying some Clousers with the more transparent Ultrahair or Super Hair in lieu of bucktail can spell success when more typical Clousers aren't working. The colors are subtle, but offer the translucency that can't be achieved with bucktail. Some colors to look at are Polar Bear, blue, smoke, grey and lavender.

Rob Jepson, another good local striper fly fisherman, uses a color combination that employs the subtle shading that real baitfish possess, going from light on the bottom to gradually darker on the back. He achieves this by using white bucktail on the bottom, followed by dun or gray bucktail over, followed by lavender on top and, of course, some Rainbow Krystal Flash thrown in. This is a very effective Clouser.

Hank Holland

Another of Rob's flies is the "Thunder Bunny," a combination of rabbit, bucktail and epoxy to create a streamer. This pattern is also in Lefty's *Saltwater Fly Patterns*. As stated before, most flies can be fished on top, middle and bottom. Rob's pattern is certainly one of these.

ROB JEPSON'S THUNDER BUNNY

Hook: Mustad #34007, size # 1/0 to #3/0 or equal

Thread: Red or fire-orange flat waxed nylon

Belly: White bucktail

Lateral Line: Pearl Krystal Flash

Back: Rabbit Zonker Strip - chartreuse or olive

Top: Chartreuse or olive bucktail

Eye: 3mm paste-on eye, yellow with black pupil

Epoxy: 5-minute

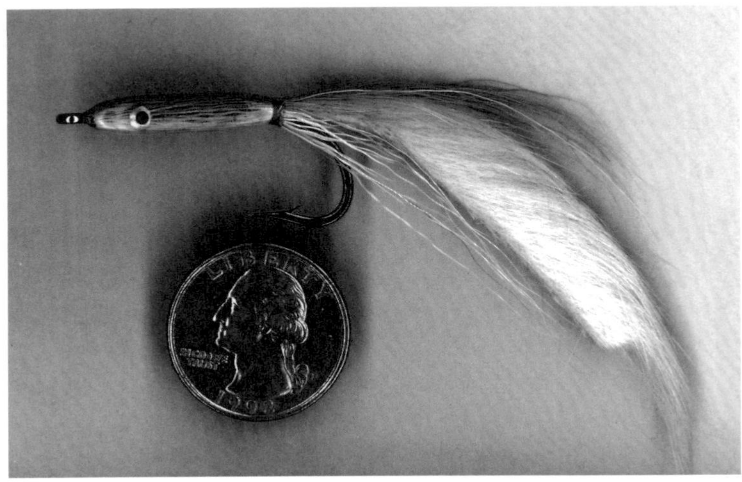

◆ TYING INSTRUCTIONS

1. Place hook in vise upside down (hook point up) and attach thread behind hook eye. Advance thread to between the hook point and barb. Remove the fur and fuzz from the zonker strip for about 1/16" from the end, and tie in with the fur side down. Advance thread to 1/4" behind hook eye.
2. Take a half pencil diameter of white bucktail and tie on shank of hook about 1/4" behind hook eye with the butts facing toward the hook point, tips extending out over the hook eye. The bucktail should be 3 to 3-1/2" long.
3. Invert hook in vise with hook point down and wrap down the bucktail to the hook eye. Advance thread to the same point that you tied in the white bucktail, and tie in a similar amount of olive or chartreuse bucktail opposite the white.
4. Tie in 6 strands of Pearl Krystal Flash and extend it beyond bend of hook 1-1/2 times the hook length.
5. Advance thread to a point between the hook barb and the point of the hook. Carefully pull back the white bucktail along the hook shank and tie down at this point.
6. Pull the olive or chartreuse bucktail down on the back of the hook shank and carefully tie off. Holding both materials in place, take several wraps around this point and tie off with a whip finish and cut thread.
7. Mix a small batch of epoxy and apply from the tie-off point to the hook eye. After the first coat has set, apply the paste-on eyes on each side of the streamer. Mix another batch of epoxy and cover the same area as before.

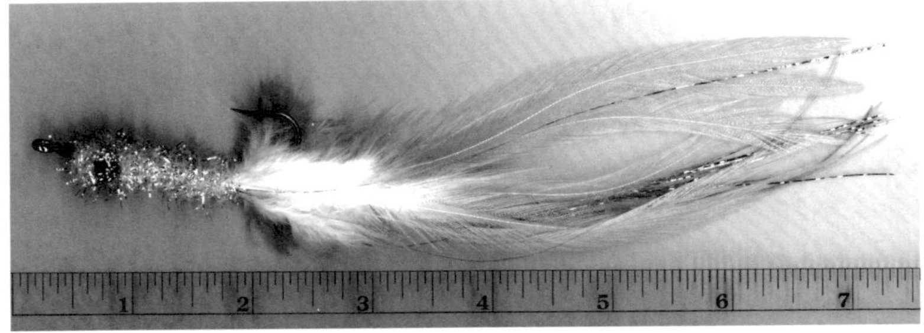

Another Lefty Kreh pattern that will bring the "big-uns" is the "Cactus Striper." The *cactus* in this case refers to the use of Flash Chenille for the body of the fly. This fly is what we call *a big fish fly,* meaning that the size of the pattern will catch the interest of the larger rockfish. By using the buggy looking Flash Chenille as the body along with the use of long saddle hackles for the tail, this fly can be tied from as short as 4 inches to as long as 8 or 9 inches. The fly is usually tied in three colors, chartreuse, white and yellow. The use of lead eyes helps turn the fly hook up like the "Clouser Minnow."

CACTUS STRIPER

Hook: Mustad #34011, size #4/0

Thread: Fire-orange flat waxed nylon

Eyes: 1/24oz plain lead barbell eyes colored with black Magic Marker

Tail: Six long saddle hackles

Tinsel: 8 to 10 strands Holographic tinsel equal amounts of silver and blue

Body: Chartreuse or pearl Flash Chenille

Colors: Chartreuse body/chartreuse tail, chartreuse body/yellow tail, pearl body/ white tail

◆ TYING INSTRUCTIONS

1. Insert hook in vise and attach thread behind hook eye. Wind thread back toward hook bend about 3/8".
2. Tie in lead eye at this point by figure-eighting around the eye and by lashing to the hook shank in front of the far eye and bringing the thread over the hook shank in front of the far eye and over the shank to the near side eye. Repeat this wrap until the eye is anchored firmly in place.
3. Advance the thread to the hook bend and prepare the 6 saddle hackles by stripping off some of the fluff. Attach three on each side of the hook shank. Length of saddles are up to you.
4. At this same point tie in the holographic tinsel on each side of the hook shank in the same spot that the saddles were attached. Extend the tinsel about 1/2" beyond the saddle tips.
5. Advance the thread to behind the hook eye. This point is between the hook bend and the back of the lead eye.
6. Tie in a 12" piece of Flash Chenille and advance the thread in front of the lead eye, between the lead eye and the hook eye.
7. Start winding the Flash Chenille to the bend of the hook and then wind back to the tie in point.
8. Next wind the Chenille over the lead eye in the same figure eight pattern that you attached the lead eye with. Make three complete passes over the lead eye on both sides. Wrap one to two wraps of Chenille in front of the lead eye and tie off with the hanging thread. Cut tag end and whip finish head.

The next two flies are crustaceans. These flies are the "crawfish" of the salt. Shrimp and crabs are great delicacies for rockfish. Sometimes they are its only food source, not because there isn't other prey around, but because they taste so good. You know how we look forward to the first corn of the year? Well, rockfish feel the same way about crabs and shrimp!

"Bruce's Crystal Shrimp" is a fast, easy and durable fly pattern that represents the saltwater shrimp found around pilings and underwater structure. This fly is tied in two sizes, since you want to match the size of food that the stripers might be feeding on at a given time. One of the least recognized aspects of this fly is the positioning of the tail material. The tail is tied with natural deer body hair on the bottom of the hook, which rides point up like the "Clouser Minnow." Tying of the lead eye on top of the hook shank causes this. This position does two things. First, it looks like the tail of a shrimp when seen from above; secondly, and most importantly, when the deer hair softens up in the water, the hair tends to flare out. This causes the fly to dart from side to side when retrieved with short strips of the line, imitating the darting motion of a real shrimp.

The three best colors of body material for striper fishing are tan, pearl and white Flash Chenille, but this pattern has had great success on redfish and speckled sea trout with rootbeer (brown/orange) and pink chenille. Bonefish also like the pearl, tan and white Flash Chenille tied on #4 & #6 hooks

BRUCE'S CRYSTAL SHRIMP

Hook:	Mustad #34007, sizes #4 & #1/0
Thread:	Fire-orange flat waxed nylon
Eyes:	1/50 oz. for #4 hooks, 1/36 oz. for #1/0 hooks. Use plain lead eye with the lighter colored chenille (tan, white, pearl) color with black Magic Marker. Use chromed plated eyes for the darker bodies (rootbeer, pink)
Antenna:	Pearl Flashabou and copper Krystal Flash-Mix four each color for #4 and six each for #1/0 hooks
Body:	Tan, pearl, white, rootbeer, pink Flash Chenille or "Estaz"
Tail:	Natural deer body hair

◆ TYING INSTRUCTIONS

1. Insert hook in vise and attach thread behind hook eye and wind back to a position between the hook point and the barb.
2. Attach lead eyes at this point by wrapping in a criss-cross winding and by lashing. Lashing is accomplished by wrapping under the lead eye and over the hook shank on both the front and back of the lead eye. Continue to do this several times to lock the eye in place. Finish between the back of the lead eye and the bend of the hook.

3. Attach the Flash Chenille at the bend of the hook and leave the chenille hanging. For #4 hook the chenille should be cut 5" and 8" for the #1/0 hook.
4. Take the proper amount of Flashabou and Krystal Flash and tie in at this point. Advance thread to back of hook eye.
5. Invert hook in vise. Straighten a small bunch of natural deer body hair and tie in with the tips extending about 1/4" beyond the hook eye. While holding the deer hair by the butts in your left hand, advance the thread and hair to behind the lead eye (in this case, behind the lead eye is the side toward the hook eye), binding down the hair as you go, keeping the material on top of the hook shank. Cut off remaining deer hair butts and advance the thread to back of the hook eye.
6. Invert hook and grasp the hanging chenille and wrap around the lead eye, criss-crossing twice around each side of the eye. Now wind the Chenille around the hook shank, advancing it toward the hook eye. Tie off behind hook eye, whip finish and apply cement.

Bruce's Crystal Crab is another fly pattern that uses the versatile Flash Chenille. Although the following pattern uses lead eyes to get the fly to the bottom, it can also be tied with plastic bead eyes and floated around structure. This works especially well at night.

BRUCE'S CRYSTAL CRAB

Hook: Mustad #34007, size #1/0

Thread: Fire-orange flat waxed nylon

Tail/craws: Natural deer body hair

Eyes: Large chain bead painted black 4 beads long

Body: Two strands of olive and one strand of tan Flash Chenille 10" long

Legs: Sililegs (silicon rubber) or green round rubber legs, 4" long

◆ TYING INSTRUCTIONS

1. Insert hook in vise and attach thread behind hook eye and wind to bend of hook.
2. Straighten a small bunch of natural deer body hair; attach at this point and let extend about 3/8" beyond hook.

3. Advance thread to middle of the hook shank, binding down deer hair as you go. Cut off remaining butts.
4. Invert hook in vise and advance thread to back of hook eye. Straighten another bunch of deer hair and tie down with the tips extending over the hook eye about 3/8", advancing thread and deer hair to the cut-off position of the other deer hair. Cut off remaining butts.
5. Invert hook in the vise to its normal position and advance thread to a point opposite the hook point. Attach one set of chain bead in the middle with two beads each extending perpendicular to the hook shank.
6. Tie in the remaining set of chain bead eyes half way between the hook eye and the first chain bead.
7. Advance thread to the bend of hook and tie in the three pieces of Flash Chenille. Leave Chenille hanging and advance thread to between the chain bead eyes.
8. Tie in two strands each of living rubber on each side of the hook shank. Advance thread to back of the hook eye.
9. Twist the hanging Flash Chenille and begin winding toward eyes. Criss-cross the chenille between one set of eyes and than do the same to the other set of eyes, being careful to not bind down the living rubber. Continue winding Chenille to back of hook eye and tie off and apply head cement.

Another crab pattern that works well on stripers (it's Lefty Kreh's favorite) is "Del Brown's Permit Fly." As the name implies, the fly was first created for permit, but it's dynamite on any saltwater fish that eat crabs. The pattern can be found in any good saltwater pattern book.

"Del Brown's Permit Fly"

Kevin Weber

Chapter 4
FISHING TECHNIQUES

Tides

Is the fishing best on the incoming tide or the outgoing? The real answer is *the best fishing is when the tide is moving and the fish are biting.*

This seems like a smartaleck answer, but there is truth in it. The influence of the tide in saltwater is equivalent to a good hatch on your favorite trout stream. Tidal movement causes the fish to feed. *Sometimes.* Although it doesn't always apply, generally the best fishing is when the tide is moving. What is the best tide? There probably isn't a perfect answer to that, as it varies depending upon where you are fishing.

An outgoing tide does do one thing that the incoming doesn't, and that is bring the food source out from cover. This exposes them to the predatory fish. Therefore, if you are fishing shoreline structure this *could* be the best tide.

What is tide? Very simply it is the effect of the moon and sun on the earth's waters. There is a gravitational pull from these bodies that causes the water to flow back and forth. Twice each lunar month the sun and moon are aligned, causing the tides to be stronger. These tides are called "spring tides," and they have the greatest height fluctuations. At the two positions in between, the gravitational forces are counteracted thus producing little tide movement. These are called "neap tides."

Checking tides before fishing an area makes good sense. If the tides are moving at low light times the fishing should be pretty good. *Sometimes.* The very best time to fish is whenever you can, but a moving tide does help.

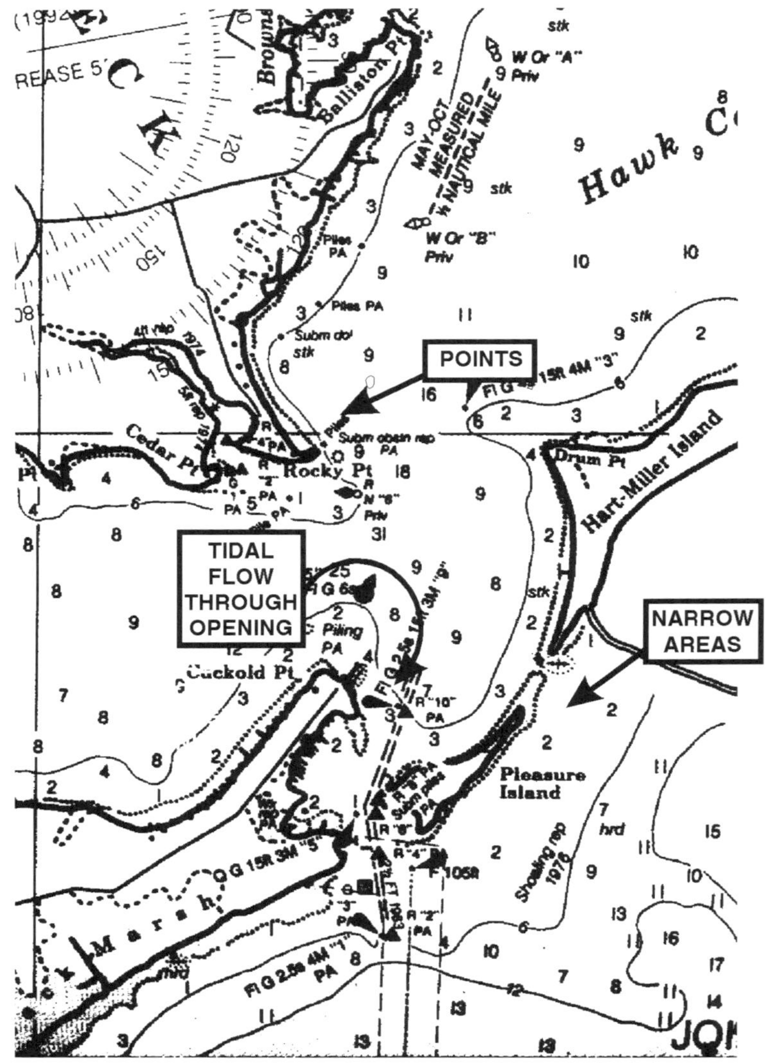

Brackish water is where freshwater and saltwater meet. Look for deep water near sharp points and tidal flow between narrow points.

Brackish Water

What is brackish water? This is where the saltwater and freshwater meet and mix. It's also where the greatest number of different fish species can be caught. Freshwater fish compete here with saltwater species for the same food source.

While fishing a brackish river off the bay one day, we caught eleven different species of fish, and actually caught six species on as many casts. Stripers are very tolerant of freshwater and sometimes a surprisingly large number of them can be found a long ways up a tributary. These waters are a great area to fish, if diversity is your thing. Again, you should pay attention to the tides. Brackish water is tidal and the fish will still respond to its movement.

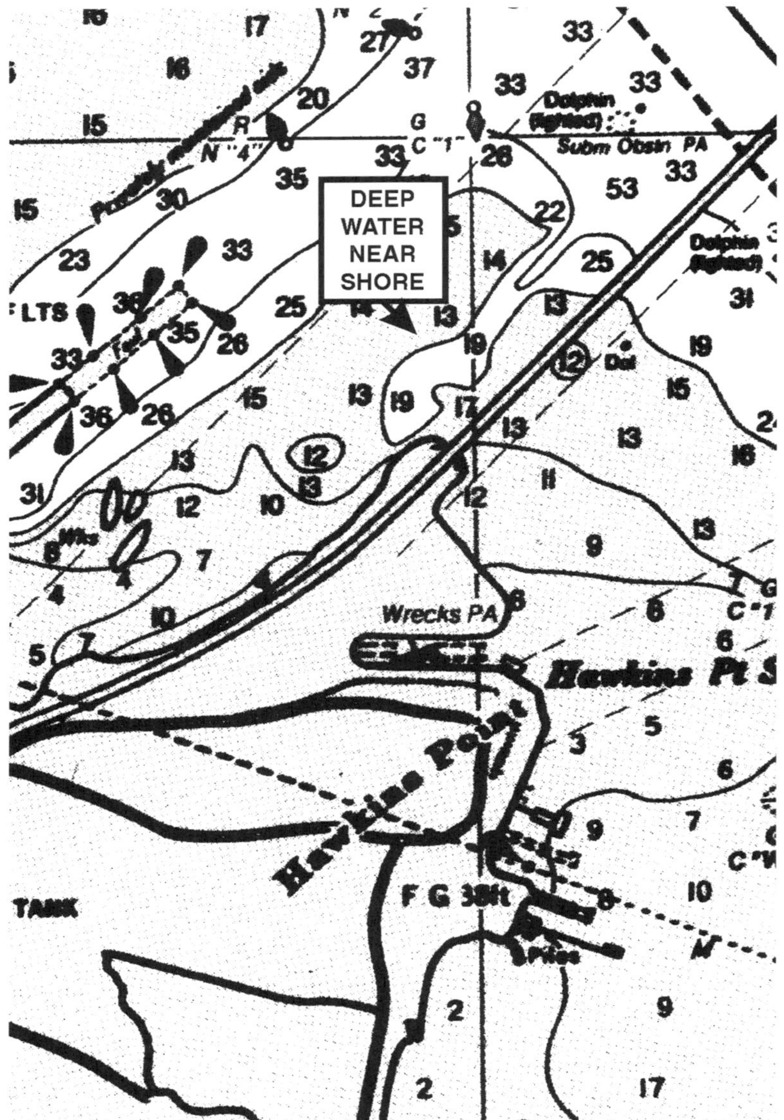

Breaking down large waters to likely holding areas are easy. Look for deep water near shore.

Where to Fish

Soon we'll talk about fishing techniques for different levels of the water column, but first let's discuss the nature of the water itself. Let's look at fishing either bays or tributaries and discover how to approach new waters for the first time.

Obviously, fishing the big waters of bays requires the use of boats to move around. *A good depth finder to locate structure and drop-offs and a good set of navigation charts* are a must. We aren't going to teach navigation techniques, but these maps are invaluable for showing the channels, underwater obstructions and depths. Learning about the waters you want to fish should begin at home. Pouring over these maps from the comfort of your easy chair will save time and effort out on the water. Also, contacting your local fishing tackle shop and asking where the fish are biting is a help. Most good shops are more than happy to provide you with this information.

Your goal is to take a large piece of water and reduce it down to the best fishing areas. What are you looking for? *You are looking for deep water close to shore.* This is the first area to concentrate on. Does this water have structure on it? Does the tidal flow cross this structure? Is the deep edge on the up-tide flow or the down-tide side? Are you getting the picture here? When you are out on the water there are things to notice. Look for boats congregated together. They aren't there to be sociable, someone found fish. Look for birds. Look for "nervous water," which is caused by baitfish close to the surface. It's usually a sign of bait being driven there by predator fish under them.

The water which is most accessible to most fishermen are the tributaries and tidal creeks off the larger waters. Here you can fish with a small car top boat, jon boat, canoe or even a float tube. There usually are some areas that can be fished on foot.

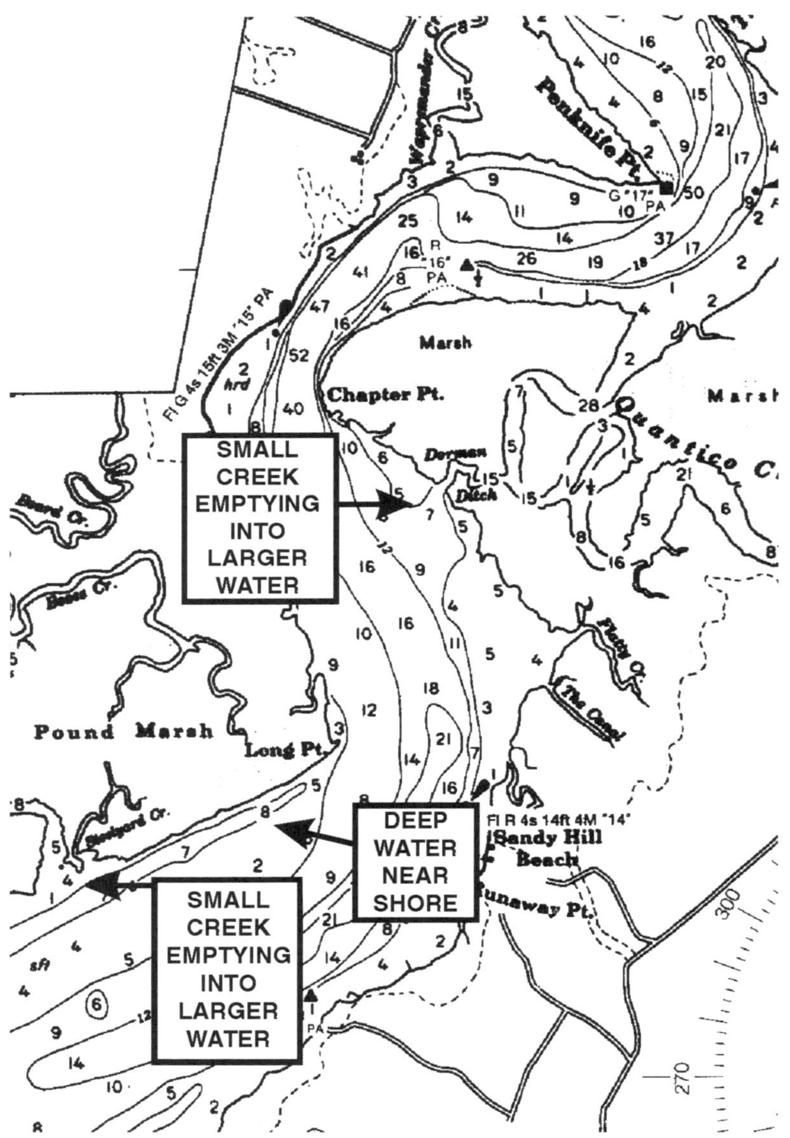

Study navigational maps for likely areas that will hold stripers. Note deep water near shore and small creeks emptying into larger water.

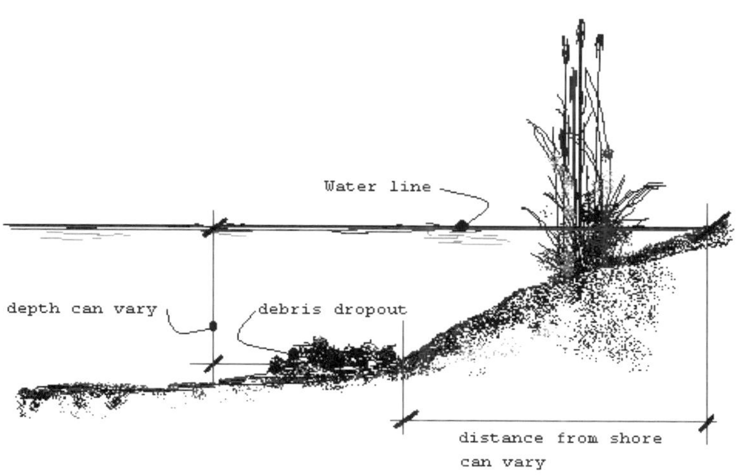

A debris line.

Where to look? The same goes here as for the larger waters, look for *deep water close to shore.* Look for piers, downed trees, rocks or other structure that is near the deep water. *This is much like going around a freshwater pond searching for bass and bluegill.* The main difference is that you are still dealing with tidal flow. No tide, no fish are biting. When you see structure in an area that has deep water close, *don't move into casting distance at first.* To do so might destroy some of the best fishing which may well be right under where you'll move your boat.

What the heck am I talking about? What I am referring to is a slight depression of debris that is deposited by both the tide and wave action against the shore. Did you ever walk out in the ocean from the beach and feel the contour of the bottom? It usually is wavy with small depressions. These are the same things that happen on the shore of tidal creeks. The leaves and small twigs and branches will become waterlogged and sink to the bottom. Wave action and tidal flow will pull or push this debris into those slight depressed contours. Over a period of time the small shrimp, crustaceans and minnows will come to use these areas for food and

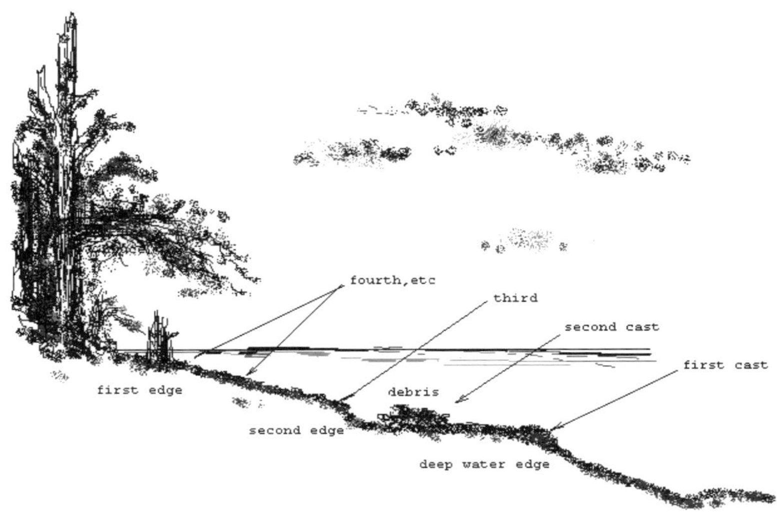

How to "work the edges."

sanctuary. They can be from a few feet off the shore to maybe twenty feet out. The depth of the drop-off usually will determine how close this edge will be, but normally there is one on any shore that can be pounded by winds.

The edges are naturally popular with the larger fish that are waiting for shrimp and minnows to be drawn there. The bait comes when a falling tide leaves their shore sanctuary bare of water. Stripers will cruise these edges, darting up the slope to take a bait and then returning to the same edge again. I have seen areas like this where the drop is extremely close to the shore, and have caught large stripers over top of the wave surge caused by a boat going by. I guess this is a tributary version of fishing the surf!

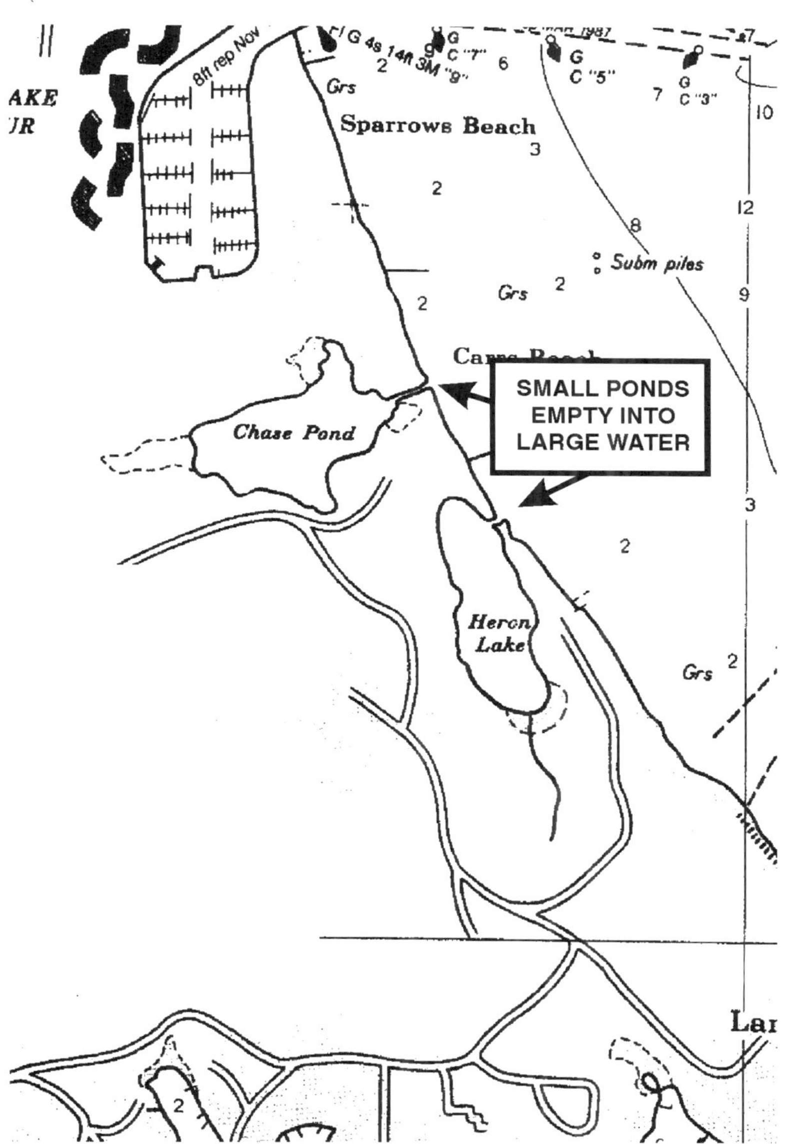

Where small ponds or creeks empty into large water are good ambush points on outgoing tides.

Where small creeks and ponds enter any larger water is another ambush point for stripers. They wait for bait to exit these waters on lowering tides. Be observant and think like the quarry you are going after.

Now let's discuss some specific fishing techniques. There are differing ways to fish different flies in different levels of the water column. We'll try to simplify things and maybe give you some new ideas.

Surface

Every fisherman loves a surface strike. Watching a fish explode on your offering is certainly one of the great thrills of fishing. Early mornings and dusk are good times to fish poppers around rocks, piers and other structures, even if there isn't much activity showing. At these times larger fish are still cruising these areas looking for a good meal, and the noise and splash of a popper will get their attention.

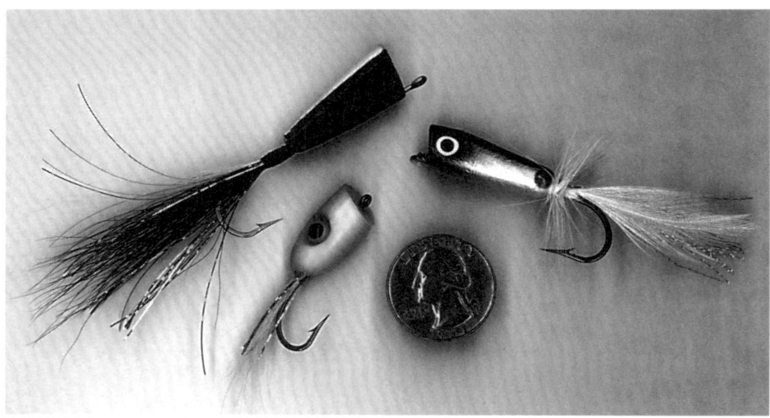

Typical surface poppers

Leaders for this type of fishing are simple, you can tie a 4 to 5-foot piece of 20 lb. test on the fly line and connect the popper to the tippet with a non-slip mono knot, or you can use the simple tapered leader described in chapter 2. Again, these fish are not leader shy. The heavy tippet material can help to stop the fish when it runs toward structure to scrape the line against sharp objects or barnacles.

Poppers are a great choice over weed beds and shallows. Stripers will hit these flies on the surface when they won't hit anything under the water at times. The fish probably thinks that the bait has seen him, by the way it's trying to escape, and this triggers the response to attack.

Although calm waters may seem like the best time to use poppers, experience teaches us that a *light chop on the water is best.* Maybe the clear water gives the fish a better look at the object on the surface and the slight broken water doesn't give the fish as clear an image.

How do you use the popper? Sometimes a continuous popping strip will bring the fish up. Sometimes a loud pop and a pause is the ticket, sometimes just a quiver on the surface will do the trick. Experiment. When one style of retrieve works keep using it until they stop hitting it, then change again. Sometimes the best popper is a slider type. These make a surface disturbance then dive under the water on the pull.

Whatever style of popper or stripping action you use, the rod should *not* be used to impart the action. The stripping hand does the work. The rod tip should always be pointed to the popper or fly. This will take the slack out of the line and allow better hook-ups when you strike the fish.

As explained before, stripers miss a popper quite a bit. If this seems to be happening too frequently for your liking, here is a trick that bass fisherman and speckled trout fisherman have used for years. They use a popper with a jig attached behind. In our case,

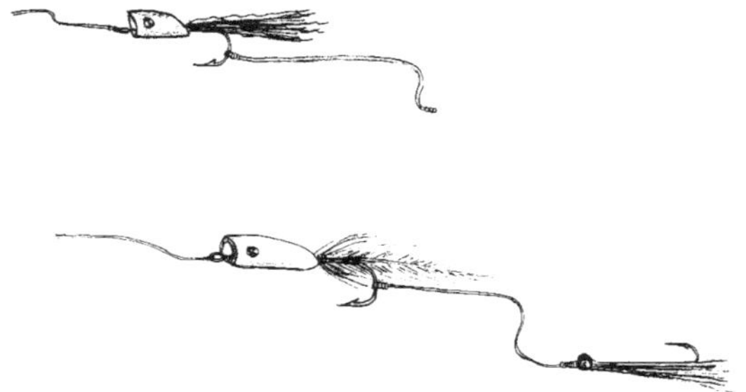

A popper and fly combination works well at times. The popper gets the fish's attention and the falling trailed fly usually is attacked.

use the popper with a fly tied behind it. This is simple rig. Simply tie an eight to fifteen inch piece of monofilament to the hook bend of the popper, and attach the fly to that. This short piece of mono will help keep the rig from tangling.

What happens is that the popper gets the fish's attention. When it sees the bait trailing behind the surface bait, it generally will attack the falling bait. What to put on behind the popper? Just about any fly that you would normally use for stripers. A slow sinking type fly or bendback style fly works well in shallow water, as does my Spoon Fly. This rig can definitely increase your hook-up rate.

Although surface fishing for stripers has maximum thrill value, it probably comprises only five percent of fishing time. That is, unless it's late summer or fall. At this time the baitfish are at their highest volume, and the striper needs to fatten up for the winter. They drive the great hordes of bait to the surface. Breaking fish can sometimes be seen all day while the tides are moving.

These breaking fish are generally in the larger tributaries and bays, thus requiring a boat to intercept the frenzy. *Don't run right up to a school*, this will put them down, instead, figure their movement and try to *get ahead of them and cut the motor and let the fish come to you.*

Throwing a popper into this melee will get some hook ups, but a fly a little under the surface will get a strike nearly every cast. A floating or intermediate line works well for flies just below the surface. My Spoon Fly, Bay Anchovy or a small Clouser or Deceiver can be used with great success. Since the fly can be seen under the surface, the strike is much like a surface strike, with all the thrills that such action brings.

Sub-Surface

How deep is sub-surface? A few inches under the surface to just off the bottom. That seems to cover a lot of territory, but in reality it doesn't. Although you can fish a fly line down below 20 feet, it isn't much fun waiting 40 seconds or more for the fly line to sink; there are far better ways to fish that depth other than with a fly rod. So, we can concentrate on levels from 20 feet up. Generally, predatory fish will be at the same level as the bait or a little under them. Check your depth finder.

As stated above, sometimes just fishing a little under the surface will bring strikes. Under breaking fish for instance, the larger fish are often under the smaller breaking fish, so fishing a sinking line can produce bigger fish. Throwing a T-300 Teeny Nymph line under a breaking school of fish, rigged with a deceiver, spoon, Clouser, etc. will produce. Use a *count down system.* Start counting when the fly hits the water; try using 5 seconds at first, then 8 on the next cast, and so on until you get a strike. Now all you have to do is use the same count, and you should be in the target range again. This is amazingly accurate, unless you get excited and can't keep up the count. This can happen to the best of us; nerves will do that to you when the water is alive with fish splashing and jumping almost in the boat.

Fishing the shallows with Lefty's Deceivers or a bendback style fly on an intermediate line during the early morning or late evening can be spectacular at times. *Again, the best areas will be bars or grass beds near the deeper water.* Also, look for sandbars or grass beds perpendicular to the tide flow. Make your cast up tide and strip the fly over the bar or grass. The stripers will be waiting down-current of the bar, waiting for the bait to come to them.

At this point, let's discuss types and styles of retrieves. These methods can be used for any sub-surface fly as well as any of the bottom bouncing patterns.

Saltwater fish actively pursue their quarry, whereas freshwater fish in a river generally wait for their food to come to them. What does this mean to a saltwater fly fisherman? It means that *speed* is often a trigger that causes the strike. The striper believes it has been seen; the bait is escaping and this triggers the take. Speed will produce this instinctive reaction, and the faster and longer that you can move the fly, the better your chances of a take. *When was the last time that you saw a baitfish slow up and let a larger fish eat him?*

Hank Holland

Figure 1: How to make a long strip. Note that the rod is pointed at the fly.

This is one of the prime reasons to use longer sinking portions of line. The longer heads will allow you to strip with greater speed, and still keep your fly in the target area.

Let's first look at a proper stance. You should be standing somewhat off-center to your casting target. This is best described as a baseball stance. This position will allow you to extend your stripping hand well behind you. You can now swim the fly over a longer distance on the pull then you could if you were facing the target. A longer pull will in turn give you the ability to apply more speed.

Hank Holland

Figure 2: The strip completed.

If you are right handed, then your left foot should be the lead foot, left handed; vise-versa. Since the body is somewhat diagonal to the casting target, you can fully extend your stripping hand behind you.

Where should the rod tip be for the retrieve? *It should always (always) be pointed at the fly.* This is of utmost importance. It takes the slack out of the fly line and allows for the best hook set. Slack line is one of the biggest reasons for lost fish, other than not having sharp hooks. The relationship of the rod tip to the water surface is another thing to consider, and this is where you can gain more movement of your fly in the water. By varying the height of the rod tip off the water, the action of the fly can be changed dramatically.

Are you wondering how that can be? When using sinking lines, the water creates a pull on them as you retrieve, because of the mass of the line itself. This pull, in turn, tugs down on the rod tip on each strip, causing it to deflect toward the line where it enters the water. The rod tip then recoils back to its straight position, causing the line to twitch and jump each time that the line is stripped.

This is one reason that fly rods are so effective. Look at what happens each time that you strip the line. Say you strip the fly six inches; first the rod tip is pulled down toward the water, the fly moves this six inches, the rod recovers to a straight position, causing the fly line to jump and twitch which causes the fly to do the same thing. Then the line, because of gravity, wants to slide under the rod tip again, causing the fly to drift for a distance. This happens every time that you move the line on a strip. This unique action cannot be duplicated with any other fishing gear.

Now that all that was said, what does it mean? It means that every time you move the fly rod tip further off the water surface, you create more movement of the fly. You can now see that because the distance between the tip and the water has increased, there is more jumping and twitching of the fly at the other end.

The effective distance from the water to the tip should range from right at the surface to about waist high. If you go any higher, you create hooking problems because the rod tip will no longer be pointing at the fly.

Hank Holland

An essential piece of equipment, a stripper basket. Note that the basket is on the hip so a long strip can be utilized.

What is the best stripping motion for rockfish? There isn't a "super strip" that will always bring a strike. The real answer is to experiment with different retrieves. Remember that one thing the striper reacts to is speed. Experiment with a fast retrieve first, with short or maybe long strips of the line. When you get a strike, try to remember the retrieve you used; keep that up as long as it works, and then try something else.

There are two retrieves that have produced more fish than others for us; *they are a "strip and kick" and a strip that I refer to as the "strip and drop."*

"The strip and kick" is accomplished by extending your rod hand from your body. Reach just behind your rod hand with your stripping hand, grasping the fly line with your thumb on top. As you strip the line to your side, at the last moment drive your thumb down with a quick snap of your hand toward the ground. This will cause the fly to lurch forward with great speed, giving the impression of a fleeing bait. This same technique has been used for years by Bob Clouser on the Susquehanna for smallmouth bass. Bob refers to it as the "Susquehanna Strip." It can be a very effective retrieve at times, and should be part of your fish catching arsenal for all species of fish.

Hank Holland

How to get that extra "kick" with your thumb.

The "strip and drop" retrieve simply requires you to pause after one strip before making the next one. How long do you pause? One-half to one second is usually enough. This retrieve makes use of a technique that has worked for decades with lead head jigs for freshwater and saltwater fish alike. It has long been known that fish will take a bait as it falls. When using a weighted fly like the "Clouser Deep Minnow," this retrieve allows the fly to do the same thing that the lead head jig does, which is to fall between strips.

Those two retrieves are just starters. Use them, and try combinations of movements and speeds. Experiment with the retrieve and remember the strip that produced a strike. When one retrieve fails, try another and then another, if all your efforts don't produce, *go home*. Just kidding; try other flies, other areas, other times, experiment and be versatile and you will be successful.

Bottom Bouncing

I've already said that fishing twenty feet deep or more with a fly rod is not what I call effective use of the equipment. Grab your spinning rod, they are made for that kind of fishing. The fly rod is one of the finest tools for stripers or any other fish, for that matter, when used in waters shallower then twenty feet. Other than the baitfish themselves, a fly made of feathers and bucktail has more movement then any hard lure ever developed. Combine this with the movement that the fly line creates as we've described, and you just can't help catching fish. . .(*usually*).

Back to the bottom; the same techniques that are used for subsurface fishing will work here. Along with bottom dwelling flies like the "Clouser Deep Minnow" and a full-sinking fly line, (see the section on lines), you have an effective combination to take stripers.

The most important aspect of fishing deep is keeping your eyes on the fly line where it enters the water. As you strip in the line, the weight of the line and fly will cause a loop between the rod tip and the line entering the water. This loop will lift and drop on each strip of the line. Anything that changes that loop size or how far it lifts off the water can only be caused by *two things*. One is a fish's lip and the other is the bottom, when in doubt, *strike*, and hope it's more often the former than the latter.

The "strip and drop" and "strip and kick" retrieves are the starting place for the bottom bouncing patterns. They will allow the fly to swim through the strip, and adding the drop or the quick kick to the fly will help trigger the strike. These retrieves will work with any deceivers, bucktails, bendbacks, etc. In the case of the weighted flies, there will be the drop at the end of the strip and, with the un-weighted flies, there will be either a quick side-to-side movement or a quick up-movement of the fly depending on the retrieve you use. We have discussed these retrieves as two different ways to add life to a fly. They can also be used together within the same retrieve to cause the fly to jump, kick, drop and swim. How does a real baitfish move? Does it have the capability of doing all of these things? Absolutely. Try to think like the bait being chased and you'll catch more fish!

Winter

Spring

Summer

Fall

Those of us that frequent *The Fisherman's Edge* determine the time of the year by the hat Joe is wearing.

Chapter 5
STRIPERS THROUGH THE SEASONS

Depending on weather conditions and access to certain waters, stripers can be caught all year around. We'll take a look at what to do during different times of the year.

Winter

Either mild winters or fast freezes can mean good striper fishing all winter. How can this be? Mild winters are obvious; baitfish will still be on the move. If the bait doesn't move, stripers won't either. How about fast freezes? When winter temperatures come on extremely quick, the smaller tributaries and shallow creeks tend to be a little warmer. This is because their dark bottoms absorb the sun's rays, causing them to heat faster and stay warmer than a larger body of water will. When this happens the larger water

Big flies can be good when the weather is cold.

becomes a cold water barrier that the bait won't cross. Therefore, the bait stays in the creeks and tributaries, and the rockfish stay also. As a rule, stripers over five pounds in our Chesapeake Bay will move out with the migrating bait when the waters start to cool. But when the temperatures drop dramatically, as they did in 1995, we can catch stripers to thirty pounds in our local creeks. This could be repeated in any body of water along the Coast if such conditions repeat themselves.

Other places to look for stripers in the winter are warmwater discharges from electrical facilities. The water at these points can be from 20 to 25 degrees warmer than the surrounding waters. This causes baitfish to congregate, and the rockfish will certainly follow. Generally during the winter months, these areas will have gizzard shad (mud shad), and in late winter blue backed herring will show up. These waters are usually deep, and require fast-sinking heads or full-sinking lines and large flies. Nine to twelve inch long flies will usually heat up the fish and may warm you up too, if you're lucky enough to have access to these waters. Although stripers usually start biting after water temperatures go over 45 degrees, they have been caught in some pretty chilly holding waters in January, if the bait is there.

Spring

When the water temperature moves above 45 degrees, the stripers begin to become active. The striper schools will start to move from their winter haunts to the shallows as they look for small minnows and grass shrimp in the shoreline debris. The larger fish

Bill May

A big man makes a 30" striper look small.

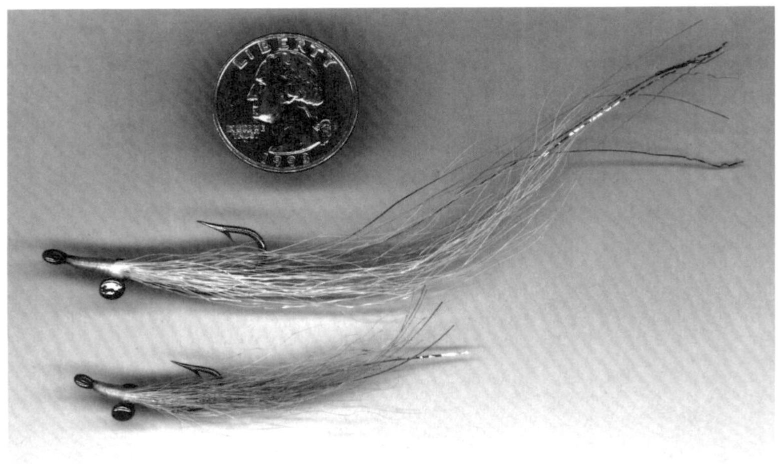

Clouser minnows mimic common baitfish.

will slowly make their way to the lower reaches of their spawning grounds, usually following the deep shipping channels.

Also, blue backed herring will start their migration into the river systems for their spawning ritual. The largest of the stripers have learned this, and will also be waiting for the migration. Large blue and pink Deceivers will imitate these baitfish very well. Any large bulky fly will get the rockfish's attention. Work them around the drops and edges of the shallow water, as well as through back eddies in the rivers. Although the stripers can be spread out over a large area during this time of year, it is also the best time to hook the largest ones of the year.

We've noted that the traditional spawning grounds will start filling with breeding fish. Again, large flies are the order of the day. Since spawning grounds are in brackish or freshwater, flies

that imitate the local fish are the logical choice. These waters harbor white perch, yellow perch, crappie, etc. A fly on the white, or certainly light-colored side, from three inches to nine inches will match this "hatch."

As a word of caution, and to emphasize good conservation practice, don't go to these areas with light rods. These fish are your future, and exhausting a large fish on light tackle is not sporting or even very smart at this point. Heavy rods, nine to 10-weight, will subdue the fish faster and allow them to spawn and roam for another day.

Summer

After the spring spawning run ends, the striper will start spreading into the main bays and tributaries. These warm waters will be filled with small baitfish and grass shrimp. Size 4 and 2 Clouser Minnows, bay anchovys and silversides will work for the smaller rockfish found here. In the middle regions of the coast this will occur around early June, and the number of stripers entering these waters will keep increasing until fall. As this increase builds, so do the size of the stripers. Many small creeks and bays will have their share of stripers in the twenty to twenty-six inch range. As the summer moves on, the stripers will start feeding more at the surface in these smaller waters, especially in the mornings and evenings. A small thin pencil popper or a "Bruce's Spoon Fly" is the ticket for these breaking fish.

Fall

Fall is a time of bounty, and is the period of fattening up for the winter months. This is the best time of the year to fish for stripers. They are more aggressive at this time of year than at any other. They will feed almost all day, as long as there is tide movement. In the large waters, there can be acres of breaking fish, feeding on silversides and bay anchovys. The tributaries will have shrimp and minnows fattening up for the winter, and the stripers will be there also eating up the fattened prey.

Events that occur in the Fall will also help you *locate* fish. What did I say? What I'm referring to is finding the back eddies whose existence becomes obvious from the congregation of fallen leaves. These will move with the tidal current, and pile up in the back eddies around small bends in the creeks or shore line. Many times these eddies aren't visible until some debris is on the water.

Fish these areas like you would a river or stream. The stripers will be hiding along these eddy lines waiting for the bait to come to them, just like a trout would in a river. Generally smaller flies will work here; Clousers or shrimp on a #4 hook are a good bet. Cast across these waters, working your fly around the heaviest concentration of leaves; this will probably be at the head or tail end of the back eddy.

Stripers will stay in the tributaries as long as the bait stays. In some areas this might be early January. As the weather cools, the bait will start migrating into the larger waters, and the stripers will be right behind them. Both are now moving to their wintering haunts, waiting for those first warming days in the early spring to start their life cycle all over again.

Bill May

Calm water, structure and a nice striper. . . what else could you ask for?

Conclusion

We sincerely hope the information that has been presented in this mini-book will help you to improve your fishing experience, but remember, there is no substitute for time on the water. The more you get out and fish, the more insight you will absorb about what the fish do at different times and under different conditions. This kind of knowledge, along with increasing your technical skills, can't help but make you a better fly fisherman!

Good luck and good fishing

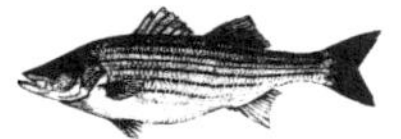